Adventure Awaits

*Harnessing Today's Potential for
God's Greater Purpose*

— JANE MERSON —

Sacristy
Press

Sacristy Press
PO Box 612, Durham, DH1 9HT

www.sacristy.co.uk

First published in 2020 by Sacristy Press, Durham

Copyright © Jane Merson 2020
The moral rights of the author have been asserted.

All rights reserved, no part of this publication may be reproduced or transmitted in any form or by any means, electronic, mechanical photocopying, documentary, film or in any other format without prior written permission of the publisher.

Unless otherwise indicated, Scripture quotations are from the ESV® Bible (The Holy Bible, English Standard Version®), copyright © 2001 by Crossway, a publishing ministry of Good News Publishers. Used by permission. All rights reserved.

Scripture taken from The Message copyright © 1993, 1994, 1995, 1996, 2000, 2001, 2002. Used by permission of NavPress Publishing Group.

Every reasonable effort has been made to trace the copyright holders of material reproduced in this book, but if any have been inadvertently overlooked the publisher would be glad to hear from them.

Sacristy Limited, registered in England & Wales, number 7565667

British Library Cataloguing-in-Publication Data
A catalogue record for the book is available from the British Library

ISBN 978-1-78959-106-4

Contents

Foreword iv

1. Created for Adventure 1
2. Beginning the Adventure 13
3. Designed for Adventure 25
4. Essential Tools for the Journey 39
5. Facing Opposition 61
6. Embracing Challenge and Change 74
7. The Waiting Game 91
8. Anticipating Adventure 113
9. Packing Light 131
10. When Adventure Becomes a Habit 142
11. The Greatest Adventure 160

Notes 179

Foreword

Sometimes in life, you have the privilege to meet someone, who from the first encounter, you recognize and sense that this person has a story, has something to say, and walks with God. Jane is that kind of person. I remember, vividly, the first time I met Jane in 2018. I sensed God's Spirit while talking with her after a service in our church plant in Frankfurt, Germany. Jane's love for God was palpable, her love for people infectious, and her authenticity was refreshing. My family and I had moved to Germany in 2013 from America. We left a fairly comfortable life to follow a clear call in our hearts to help facilitate church planting and raise up leaders in Germany. That said, my wife and I were hardly sure how our story would unfold, but we knew it would definitely be an adventure! When talking to Jane that first night, I sensed that radical obedience and profound trust in God. Jane's own willingness to follow God and take risks in the face of insecurities and fears is one, with which people like you and I can identify. Jane has a story to tell. Jane has a story to tell that can spark hope and give encouragement in your own walk with God. When I think about Jane, my mind races back to centuries before to a passionate and devoted group of Christ-followers who left their homeland to follow God's Spirit and embark on an adventure.

The Celtic missionary movement is one highlight of Christian history in Europe in the first six hundred years or so after Christ. The Celtic missionaries' lifestyle was described in Latin as *peregrinatio* or translated as wandering or traveling. However, they were hardly "wanderers" in the sense of a directionless, helpless, or forlorn people; they were pilgrims, followers of Christ inspired and called by God to travel, preach, and make disciples. These Celtic missionaries were committed followers of Christ, and they trusted in the Holy Spirit's divine direction. They had a passion to share their faith and were captivated by eternity and a heavenly home. They were travelers, in that they had a missionary spirit and radical obedience. They were a movement of normal people who simply said "Yes" to God. Wherever the Spirit would lead them, they were willing to follow. When I think about their radical obedience and the heart of these Celtic missionaries, I hear echoes of Jane's story. Or perhaps, it is within Jane's story, in which I see the same passion and zeal of the Celtic missionaries.

In Acts 13, we find Paul and Barnabas participating in a powerful worship gathering. During this meeting, God's Spirit clearly speaks to the gathering and tells them to send out Paul and Barnabas. They started their adventure. The same Spirit of God, who spoke during that powerful worship gathering, is the same Spirit which has led and guided Jane through the years. She shares eloquently and inspirationally calling us all higher and into a beautiful trust in following Christ. Sometimes, you will hear the whispers and providential guidance of the Spirit in Jane's story, and at other times, you will witness God's Spirit clearly leading Jane. Part of what makes Jane's story so compelling, is that she does not gloss over her own challenges. Her story is not one simply sharing the joys of following God's Spirit, wherever he was leading her. Your heart will be moved and stirred as you read not only the joys of her story but also the times of difficulty, waiting, breaking, and learning to trust. Paul and Barnabas had to trust God's Spirit as they launched out and began their adventure. The Celtic missionaries did several hundred years later. Jane shares her story of learning to trust and follow the leading of the Holy Spirit.

The first time that I read Robert Frost's poem in school, "The Road Less Traveled", something deep from within longed to find that road—the one less traveled. However, I did not know at that time, but that was actually the Spirit of God beginning a work in me. He was preparing me for what was to come. Jane is also one of those people, who has found that road. But in reality, it is the road of Christ-followers through the centuries—people who have been willing to take up their cross and follow Christ on the narrow road. This is Jane's story—one of willingness to risk and experience life to the full in God. Her story resonates with normal people like you and me because she walks you through her fears, challenges, pain, and trust, while still beckoning you to embark on a trust-filled journey in Christ.

My life is richer and fuller from knowing Jane individually—as one adventurer to another. Jane's own story is not prescriptive but full of raw, powerful, biblical and authentic life lessons. God is raising up a new generation of passionate, committed, grounded, risk-taking, adventurers, who are going to ignite a new movement both within and outside the Church. Jane is one of those people. Some of these risk-takers will stay, where they are and make an impact on society for Christ. Others, like Jane, maybe called to go to other places and lands. Currently, I have the amazing privilege of serving together with Jane in the same church—and I am sooo blessed to have that honor! Jane is part of this generation, which are willing to risk and follow God's Spirit. Jane's story embodies it, and her story will inspire you. Her story will encourage you about who God is. The life lessons will motivate you to not allow your own fears and inhibitions to hold you back but to learn to trust Christ—wherever and however he leads you. Your story is not Jane's story or my story. However, through Jane's story, you will hear the still small voice of the Holy Spirit whispering that an *Adventure Awaits*.

Brian Weaver
Lead Pastor of New Life Church
Frankfurt, Germany

1

Created for Adventure

Just before my youngest brother graduated from university, I called him one afternoon for a chat. We had not talked for a month or two, and, being his (only) protective big sister, I like to get the lowdown on all his recent endeavours, challenges and misdemeanours. Plus, of course, hear the latest on his love life.

As we chatted that afternoon, weaving between the trivial and more serious topics of conversation, we inevitably found ourselves discussing his possible next steps and his greater hopes for the future. We talked around a number of different ideas—some very "normal", others a little more radical. With my big-sister-know-it-all approach still very much in play, I insisted on sharing a few of my own more traumatic life choices and offered him some advice that I wish I had adhered to back in the day. Finally, having heard enough of my common sense, he implored, "But life is an adventure!"

An adventure, eh? The dictionary defines adventure as an exciting or unusual experience; a bold, usually risky undertaking; a hazardous action of uncertain outcome.[1]

Do these words accurately describe your life? Perhaps for some, but I doubt, for the rest of us, that the words "risky" or "uncertain" are the first that come to mind. Yet if they were to describe your life, how would that make you feel? A few years ago, the very idea of considering life as a risky undertaking of uncertain outcome would have had me breaking out in cold sweats. So, do you need to go and lie down, or have I captured your attention?

Depending on our attitude, we may think life is something that happens to us, or else that life is something we build for ourselves. Sometimes, we may misunderstand how the world works and think that

God, or others, play us like puppets for their own personal gain. Perhaps we feel trapped by our circumstances and it takes all of our strength just to make it through another day. In reality, life is a bit of both: reaction and proaction. Our life is the result of every one of our decisions, choices and plans. But upon what, or whom, do we base these things?

Oswald Chambers, an early-twentieth-century evangelist and teacher, born in my home city of Aberdeen in Scotland, once stated, "As Christians we are not here for our own purpose at all. We are here for the purpose of God, and the two are not the same."[2] Yet, throughout our lives, beginning at a very young age, we are invited to dream dreams for our future. We ask toddlers what they would like to be when they grow up. We ask children in school to select subjects and courses based on their desired career choices. As we get older, decisions based around relationships and family become more commonplace. Then thoughts turn to retirement and how we wish to spend our final years on earth. But how often do we ask God what *he* has in mind for us?

When we map out the life we want, we usually fall into one of two camps: the first is where I pitched my tent for the first twenty-odd years of my life. This camp is regulated and controlled, every detail carefully anticipated and prepared for. Here, we play it safe, reluctant to take any risks, ensuring that we remain in control of our circumstances as far as possible and not allowing our circumstances to control us. This is where society generally expects us to be; we look the part, act the part, speak the part and blend in with the crowd. If we have a relationship with God, we pray to him and read his Word faithfully but often struggle to accept his promises for our own lives when he does not immediately provide a detailed roadmap to take us there. In this camp, we place God as our Companion, not our Conductor.

The second camp is where all the daredevils live (and sometimes my youngest brother). Here, everything is spontaneous; we live for thrills and surprises. We live recklessly, taking risks with little concern for the consequences of our actions. We want to experience life in its fullest but do so in our own way: travelling, meeting lots of people, hopping from place to place, job to job, with little concern for responsibility and commitment. Here, if we know God, we may jump at every exciting opportunity that comes our way and look to him only when the aftermath is too much for us to handle. In this camp, God becomes our Guardian, not our Guide.

When we fail to live in the fullness of God's will and purpose for our lives, we get stuck in one of these two camps and we do not permit God to map out our journey through life. We often associate idolatry with money, fame or power, but there are many more subtle idols that sneak into our lives too. It can be very easy to slip into idolatry and be unaware of it. John Piper, an American pastor and author, said: "We make a god out of whatever we find most joy in. So find your greatest joy in God and be done with all idolatry."[3]

For many years I was blissfully unaware that I had made control an idol. As long as I remained in control over my job, my future plans, my finances and my belongings, I was happy. I expended much time and energy in seeking to build a sense of control in my life, and therefore fabricating feelings of peace and comfort. "Normality", routine, convention made me happy. Or so I thought.

Perhaps it is something different for you. What makes you happy? Is it comfort? Or security? Even adventure can become an idol if that is where we look to find our joy. Perhaps we crave it so much that we begin to exaggerate our circumstances and blow everything out of proportion, just to feel like we are in one. Instead, however, we ought to seek first the kingdom of God and his righteousness, and then all these other things will be given to us as well (Matthew 6:33).

Fortunately for us, God is a gracious God and, if we repent of our own way of doing things, he will lead us into a far greater adventure. The Bible teaches that God is a sovereign God, for many are the plans in the mind of a person, but it is the purpose of the Lord that will stand (Proverbs 19:21). To some, this may seem stifling and controlling, but what we often fail to understand is that the Lord's purposes *are* the greatest adventures! In the Gospel of John, Jesus stated, "I came that they may have and *enjoy* life, and have it in abundance [to the full, till it overflows]" (John 10:10b (AMP) emphasis added).

Life should neither be a chore nor a great burden: Jesus said himself that it is to be *enjoyed*! The reason he came as a man to earth to die and to take the punishment for our sin is so that we can live a life free from guilt, shame and fear, and instead live a full, rich life in freedom. Jesus *wants you* to have fun.

Now, I am not talking about the kind of temporary fun had on a night out that fills us with regret the next morning. (Or, if you are an introvert like me, you might prefer an evening on the couch watching a movie.) These things may be all well and good in and of themselves, but real fun and joy are found in living a life of faith in the purposes that God created us for. Nothing is more exciting than entering into an adventure with God at the helm.

When we live a life that places God as our Captain, our lives *will* become an adventure: it's a guarantee. It *will* be filled with excitement and inexplicable experiences, but also much risk and uncertainty. And though we may be buffeted by the waves through stormy seasons, God has never failed to navigate his children safely out the other side. There is a vast ocean of uncharted waters before us; we need only allow the Heavenly Captain to plot the course. A life full of excitement, anticipation, thrills and the abundant testimony of his goodness and faithfulness awaits us if we choose his adventure.

In God's plan for our lives, he calls on us to chase dreams, take risks and step out into the unknown. But the best part of an adventure with God is that your dreams can never exceed the plans that he has for you. When we surrender everything to him and to his will and purpose for us, listening to his voice and walking in obedience to him, every day will become an adventure.

It is no accident that you are sitting reading this book right now. It is not by chance that it has made its way into your hands during the season that you are in. No matter what you are facing this week or this month—good or bad—God can use it to mould you and prepare you for his purposes. All your mountain-top experiences, all your struggles in the valleys of life, are invaluable tools and lessons in the adventure that God wants to take you on.

God uses every experience, every mistake, every regret, every hurt, to prepare you for his purposes and to reveal his glory to the world in which you live. Too many people live merely adequate lives while nursing a restless heart: a heart that God created for adventure.

I love to watch movies. Depending on my mood, I will watch a range of genres, including comedy, romance, science fiction and action. However, some of my favourite movies, like *The Blind Side*, *Hidden Figures* and *Apollo 13*, are those based on true stories. I sit, mesmerized, watching dramatizations of real-life heroes who have taken great risks, faced adversity and tremendous challenges, but, against all the odds, have overcome. The heart of humanity loves to hear tales of victory and survival; why else would these stories be considered enthralling enough for Hollywood to come a-knocking? Because they instil *hope*. Hope that if they can do it, so can we. Hope that, no matter what difficulties we face, we can overcome.

Yet, I think that in amongst the hope that arises within us following the retelling of survival tales, fear also flickers through. We ask ourselves, what would I do if I were in their situation? Could I really do what they did? Do I have what it takes? And doubt begins to cloud our vision. But is it not about time we stopped watching everyone else's adventures and started living our own?

If you could do absolutely anything, what would it be? How would you make a difference in the world if you had unlimited resources and a global and influential network of people? Maybe you would build an orphanage for children caught in poverty, or open a half-way house to support ex-addicts settling back into society after rehabilitation. Perhaps you would start an organization to fight injustice, or set up a scheme to befriend and support the elderly in your community. It could be that you hold a dream to compete at the Olympics, or open a Fairtrade coffee shop, or make a medical breakthrough. What has God shown to you and given you an unquenchable desire to achieve?

Now consider this: is God sovereign? Does he not have unlimited resources at his fingertips? Is he not the ultimate networker and promoter? Is it not in his power to make those dreams a reality?

You're maybe nodding as you read this, but in your heart you are still thinking, "That is all very well for others, but who am I that God would use me?" Yet God planted those dreams in your heart for a reason. He does not just want you to *dream* those dreams, he wants to make them a reality in your life. He wants to take you on the adventure of a lifetime to see those dreams *fulfilled*; this will not only benefit others, but cause you to grow, teach you to become the person he made you to be and, most importantly, bring himself glory so that the world will see the goodness of God in a tangible way.

The Gospel of John reminds us that we did not first choose God, but he chose us and appointed us to live our lives in such a way that points the world to Jesus (John 15:16a). Meditate on that for a minute. God *chose* us. God chose *you*. He imagined you, made you, grew you and shaped you, and he has appointed you to bear spiritual fruit in this world. We sometimes doubt ourselves, don't we? We think, "Why would God choose me? What difference could I really make?" The world is so big, and we are so small. But we often forget that we have the Greatest Ally in this war for the world!

God has a specific purpose that he has created you for and prepared you for: to show you his power and so that his name may be proclaimed in all the earth (Exodus 9:16).

The world would lead us to believe that we are defined by culture, race, fashion choices, size, social standing, wealth or religion; in actual fact, we are defined by our Creator, God. He intricately and uniquely designed each of us and knitted us together in our mother's womb (Psalm 139:13). He knew every step we would take on our journey before we even knew how to walk (Psalm 139:16). He offers to empower us, giving not a spirit of fear, but of power, of love and of self-control (2 Timothy 1:7). And he equips those who choose to walk in his ways with gifts (1 Peter 4:10) to help us complete the unrivalled race that has been set out before us (Hebrews 12:1).

Forget where you have been and consider where you are going. It is what is ahead that matters, not what is behind. When we give God everything, he can restore all that has been broken, hurt or lost. We find our true identity in God, our Heavenly Father, not in our own, earthly circumstances.

Your history may state, "I don't love you," but God says, "I have loved you with an everlasting love" (Jeremiah 31:3). The words, "you were a mistake," may haunt your thoughts, but God intricately wove you together from your conception (Psalm 139:15–16); before he formed you in the womb he knew you (Jeremiah 1:5). Perhaps you were told, "you will never make anything of yourself", but God declares, "I have plans to give you a future and a hope" (Jeremiah 29:11). People might have rejected you, but God whispers, "You, yes *you*, are my treasured possession" (Exodus 19:5). Your circumstances may cause you to believe you are alone, but God has promised, "I will never leave you nor forsake you" (Hebrews 13:5).

God has more in mind for your life than you could ever imagine; you need only surrender it to him. God can and will do unimaginable things with a surrendered life: just allow him the chance to show you. Give him everything and you will find yourself living a Hollywood-worthy adventure every single day. The Bible promises that no eye has seen, nor ear heard, nor any human heart imagined, what God has prepared for those who love him, in this life or the next (1 Corinthians 2:9).

All too often we settle for what is visible and believable because we can only see as far as our own abilities will take us. But God wants to expand our scope to see with eyes of faith, beyond the natural and into the realm of the supernatural. His plan for our lives is far beyond anything we could ever hope for or imagine. He is looking for men and women who are ready to partner with him to do the impossible. If we are willing, he will take us on our own unique, heaven-prepared adventure where miracles and surprises become the norm.

One of the most important lessons I have learnt over the past ten years is not to dismiss "crazy" dreams. Being a natural problem-solver, my brain automatically begins to map out a path to success when an idea or dream is presented—I can't help myself. But sadly, some ideas proposed to me were never realized because, in my limited understanding, I failed to join all the dots in my mind and therefore dismissed the dream as obsolete. I depended only on my own abilities and forgot to include God's unmatched power in the equation. You see, when you dream dreams that have a defined path to success, you will rest within the boundaries of your own abilities. But I have learnt that if you begin to dream dreams that seem utterly impossible—ridiculous, some might say—for the glory of God, it becomes a necessity to depend on him every single step of the way. And in doing so, you simultaneously step into adventure.

Yet as we advance forward, there's an enemy trying to hold us back. The earlier part of John 10:10 reads, "The thief comes only to steal and kill and destroy . . . " What is he coming to steal, kill and destroy? Every dream and promise that God has placed in your heart. The enemy, Satan, is out to discourage you and distract you from the great adventure that God wants to take you on. He does not want us to chase our destiny, knowing full well that he does not stand a chance against us when we surrender to God and begin to operate in the power that God makes available to us by his Spirit. Instead, the enemy seeks to blind us with doubt and fear, or distract us with lies, convenience and instant pleasures. One of his greatest weapons, however, is that of comparison.

Sadly, this world breeds comparison and competition like rodents in heat. In the media, we are bombarded with "before" and "after" photographs of makeovers and weight-loss success stories. Within our workplaces, success is more often determined by the title on our email footer or the number of zeros printed on our payslip each month. We are encouraged to strive to acquire the latest car model, the longest driveway or the most exotic holiday. I think we have become so accustomed to a competitive mentality that we fail to notice it when it creeps into our churches too.

Some of us might want to serve in the ministry that has the best T-shirts or the fanciest badges because we are already imagining how they might look on our next social media post, eager to clock up a great response. Perhaps we want to be noticed in our roles and therefore seek to join the ministries that are more visible within the church or are present on stage, but jealousy catches up with us when others are recruited and we are not. By comparing ourselves to others and seeking out opportunities for our own selfish ambition, we will blur our understanding of God's call on us as individuals.

Don't misunderstand me; serving in these teams is a good thing and many of us are called to serve the local church in this way. But we must be careful not to allow our attitudes and motives to become corrupted. Not all ministry can be identified by a team name or T-shirt design. These opportunities are just the tip of the iceberg.

When we understand that we were created individually to serve a unique purpose in God's great story for humanity, we no longer feel the need to compare ourselves to others because we recognize that no-one else can fulfil the role that God has created us for. It is our responsibility to lead the life that the Lord has assigned to each of us, and to which God has called us (1 Corinthians 7:17).

The story of Jesus' birth is probably the best-known biblical narrative in history. Whether or not individuals, nations or religious groups accept it as truth, most are still familiar with the Christmas story and the young woman, Mary.

She was just a teenager when the Angel Gabriel appeared to her in her home and announced that she would conceive a son by the Holy Spirit. When the angel told her that she had found favour with God and would give birth to the Son of God, her response was staggering: "I am the servant of the Lord; let it be to me according to your word" (Luke 1:38).

This single moment would define Mary's life. The angel had presented her with a declaration of God's favour upon her, a promise of what would be, and a special purpose for her to fulfil. But she had a choice. She could have walked away from what seemed to be a terribly big responsibility. Or she could step forward in faith into the purpose she had been created for. It was no accident that the angel had visited her; she was not selected at random, nor was she the second or third choice because other teenage virgins had said no. God chose her because she had found favour with him, and she had been born and strategically placed to play a key role in the salvation of humankind!

On the one hand, she was engaged to be married to a good man who would provide for her and ensure her survival. In those days, women were entirely dependent on male relatives to give them a home and to supply their needs. If she accepted the word of the Lord, she would certainly be subject to shame and rejection from those closest to her. She would likely lose her betrothed when he found out that she was pregnant, and then what? How would she provide for herself and her baby then? But, what if . . . ? What if she accepted this God-ordained task . . . ? What if she took a deep breath, and shot up a quick prayer to her Heavenly Father? "God, if this really is what you want me to do, give me the strength and grace to see it through. I don't know how to walk this path, but I trust you to lead me and provide for me every step of the way."

Mary chose what would be the more difficult road, but by choosing to walk in the purpose that God called her to, she gained a front-row seat to Jesus' life on earth. She witnessed miracle after miracle and had the incredible responsibility and awesome privilege of raising the Son of God. She became a passenger on the greatest adventure anyone could dream of because she believed that "nothing will be impossible with God" (Luke 1:37).

But there is another character in the Christmas story who also encountered an angel of God: a minor character who was not so quick to believe the words spoken over him. His name was Zechariah.

Zechariah was a priest in Judah and was married to Elizabeth, a relative of Mary. They lived their lives in a way that was pleasing to God, but they had no children because Elizabeth was unable to conceive.

As Zechariah was going about his usual business in the temple one day, the angel appeared to him and told him that Elizabeth would become pregnant and they would have a son. He was to be called John (who would later be known as John the Baptist) and would play a special role in God's great plan for humanity. But Zechariah doubted the promise spoken by the angel and questioned the likelihood of a couple of their age being able to conceive.

The angel answered him, "I am Gabriel. I stand in the presence of God, and I was sent to speak to you and to bring you this good news. And behold, you will be silent and unable to speak until the day that these things take place, because you did not believe my words, which will be fulfilled in their time" (Luke 1:19–20). Because of his doubt, Zechariah remained mute until his son was born nine months later, but he learnt a valuable lesson and still lived to see the fulfilment of God's promise to him.

Neither Mary or Zechariah were anyone particularly important or distinguished in the world before God spoke promise and purpose over their lives. They had been going about their usual daily routine when God stopped them in their tracks and set them on a greater path. Yet they were willing to be interrupted by God to step into a higher purpose. They were willing to let go of their own plans and allow God to write their story. Similarly, we do not need to seek out a big conference or special worship event to meet with Jesus; we simply need to have open and receptive hearts as we go about our day.

No matter who you are—your age, stage of life, profession, marital status or whatever—you have the opportunity to enter into a greater adventure. You don't need to take a gap-year, travel the world or have a bottomless pit of money: just enter into the best, the optimum, the too-good-to-be-true life of faith that God invites you to participate in. Every single day can be lived to a greater potential when surrendered into the hands of God. Relinquish control, surrender your plans, and ask him where he wants to take you, what he wants to achieve through you and who he has called you to be. Your adventure can begin today.

One of my favourite passages in the Bible is Hebrews 11, because it lists name after name after name of people who lived a life of faith, just like Mary. It is, essentially, God's Hall of Fame (or God's Hall of Faith, as I like to call it). It highlights just a handful of the great men and women who entered into a faith-filled adventure with God, taking risks and witnessing the impossible because of their courage and resolute trust in him.

We think of the biblical greats like Moses, Abraham, the Apostle Paul and others, as heroes of the faith and those who will have the highest honour in heaven. But why can we not also be heroes of the faith in our own generation? God is the same God now as he was then. We, too, can seek after communion with God, just like the great biblical heroes and heroines did. We, too, can nurture a close, loving relationship with him. We, too, can surrender our own desires, and instead choose to walk in obedience to God and watch our faith grow as we learn to depend on him a little more each day.

Just like Mary, just like the names listed in Hebrews 11, and just like all the others God has used throughout history, he calls us—just ordinary people—into his extraordinary purposes. We simply need to hear the call and respond.

Many years ago, I scribbled in my Bible a simple yet powerful reminder to myself at the foot of Hebrews 11: "By faith, Jane . . . " It initiates a powerful response in me and causes my faith to rise every time I glimpse it because it represents my response to God's call on my life. It is a battle cry that coaxes me forward in my journey, willing me to take risks and dream big dreams; this cry acknowledges that a life dedicated to God is often filled with trials and difficulties but, nonetheless, I stand resolute in representing my Saviour and bringing his love into this dark world.

Living out your adventure does not necessarily mean you have to move to another country, go into full-time ministry or sell all your possessions (though God will ask some of us to do just that). Living out your adventure is doing whatever God calls you to do, with radical faith, trusting him in *everything*, not depending on your income, or your job, or your home, or your family, or anything for your own security. It means allowing God to give you a fresh perspective every single day, so he can open your eyes to new opportunities to trust him and to serve him. Everyone can live the adventure that God has for them, because his call also comes with all the strength and grace that we will require; we just need to ask for it. And with every surrendered life, God can do something radically different. Just like no two stories are the same in the hands of an author, no two lives are ever the same in the hands of God, the great author of time. So let's not get caught up in comparison but, instead, celebrate the diversity and creativity of God. Let's not get distracted by our own selfish ambition but, rather, stick to the course that God sets out before us. And as long as we stay within the will of God, we will live the greatest adventure available to us.

I don't know about you, but I would rather experience a life of adventure than maintain an existence of convenience. I am no longer interested in my own mediocre plans for my life or the minute dreams that I once considered achievable. I will no longer allow fear to scare me into settling for a life less than the one I am capable of living. I am ready to embrace the unimaginable, believe the impossible, and step into the destiny that God created me for.

We do not need to know where the journey will lead in order to join the path. Entering into an adventure with God is not about focusing on the destination; it requires us to trust him and see where the journey takes us. He may have allowed you to glimpse the landmarks you'll see along the way, but the unknown, hidden surprises are the parts worth waiting for!

Our Heavenly Father longs for us to enter into the adventure he has prepared for us: a life of beauty, risk, faith and miracles. Are you ready to step into your destiny? Have you packed your bags for the thrill of a lifetime? Come now, adventure awaits.

2

Beginning the Adventure

In 2011, I visited California, and the United States, for the very first time. I had gone to Redding to visit a friend and spent ten great days exploring on foot, reading in coffee shops and driving a stretch of the west coast in an electric blue Ford Mustang convertible (a particularly noteworthy upgrade from the beige Toyota Corolla I had paid for).

One day, while my friend was in school, I walked alone along what had become a familiar route: across the main street from where we were staying, down the path behind some rather grand houses, along the Sacramento River trail and across the Sundial Bridge. It was January, yet uncharacteristically warm for that time of year, and the sun was setting in the late afternoon.

As the golden light flooded the expanse ahead of me, it lit up the impressive mountains surrounding the city. I am a sucker for a sunset, so I let it envelop me like a warm hug from heaven. As I stood there admiring God's stunning creation—the snow-topped Cascade Mountain Range, the pink and orange hues painted across the sky, the sunlight shimmering on the river—my eyes filled with tears of joy and adoration. "It's beautiful!" I exclaimed upward. And quietly, unexpectedly, God whispered into my heart, "You are even more beautiful."

This was the first time I recall God speaking directly to me about his love for me. I knew he loved me, but for a very long time I had believed that we were all given a base-level measure of love, and our behaviour on earth determined how much more of God's love we could earn. It took me a very long time to accept that this was a lie. The truth is, we are extravagantly loved by God with a full-and-running-over measure of love, and no amount of good works or obedience can earn us more.

When we humble ourselves to hear what God says about us and, more importantly, *believe* what he says about us, we gain a whole new perspective. And as we begin to accept who he has made us to be, we also begin to believe that he is able to do the impossible through us.

Our parents do not wait until we are fully grown and mature before they love us: they love us from the start. They enjoy watching us learn and develop, they present us with challenges to encourage our growth, and they only give us responsibility when they feel that we are ready for it. Similarly, our Father in heaven loves us from the start, with all of our issues, problems and immaturity. He is patient with us and only allows us to face challenges or asks us to deal with sin when he knows we are ready. He overwhelms us with his acceptance before he prompts change. Just as a six-year-old is not expected to do the weekly grocery shop or prepare a family dinner, God does not place impossible expectations on us until we have the faith to see them through.

To embark on an adventure with God, first we need to know God. We need to experience who he is for ourselves and invite him to take an active part in our lives. Who is God to you? A rarely-thought-about deity that you turn to when life gets really tough? Someone to blame when things go wrong? A holy figurehead who resides in churches and gets your casual attention at Christmas and Easter? Or do you recognize him as the God who created you, formed you, loves you and wants the best for you?

The Bible states clearly that God loves humanity so much that he gave his only Son, Jesus Christ, to die a horrific death on a wooden cross. Jesus took upon himself the punishment—that is, death—for all the sin and evil in our lives so that everyone who believes in him and accepts his free gift of grace and forgiveness will not suffer the consequences of sin, but receive the promise of an eternal relationship with God, one of freedom and peace, far beyond mortal life on earth (see John 3:16).

The Bible tells us:

> Just as [Adam, in the Garden of Eden] did it wrong and got us in all this trouble with sin and death, [Jesus] did it right and got us out of it. But more than just getting us out of trouble, he got us into life! One man said no to God and put many people in the wrong; one man said yes to God and put many in the right.

> All that passing laws against sin did was produce more lawbreakers. But sin didn't, and doesn't, have a chance in competition with the aggressive forgiveness we call *grace*. When it's sin versus grace, grace wins hands down. All sin can do is threaten us with death, and that's the end of it. Grace, because God is putting everything together again through the Messiah, invites us into life—a life that goes on and on and on, world without end.
>
> Romans 5:18–21, The Message

It is because of Jesus' sacrifice that we can appear blameless before God; he has bridged the separation that sin created between us and God so that we can know him personally. God has prepared an incredible future for each of us—plans for hope and adventure and miracles—and he hears us when we pray to him. Jeremiah 29:13 promises, "You will seek me and find me, when you seek me with all your heart."

I began my relationship with God at the tender age of eight years old. My parents had taken me to church every week for as long as I could remember, and it was a core part of our family life. I remember hearing many of the well-known stories in the Bible: Noah's ark, Joseph and his multicoloured coat, Daniel in the lion's den. I realized I knew plenty *about* God, but I did not yet know him personally. I wanted to, but I had a lot of questions.

I am fairly certain I used to torment my Sunday school teachers with my constant questioning. My young heart believed all that I had heard about God, and it wanted to know God more and receive the free gift that Jesus had conquered death to give me, but I did not understand how. How do you accept Jesus' free gift of salvation? How do you get to know God as a friend, and not just a distant deity described on the pages of a book? Though I do not recall any of the responses I received (and there were many, due to my incessant inquiring), I do remember my lack of satisfaction at the answers provided.

Then one night, as I lay in bed, I decided to talk directly to God about it: a simple prayer of tender innocence, but one that was powerful and heartfelt all the same. Silently, my heart called out to the God I had heard so much about, asking him to forgive me for the naughty things I had done in my short life, declaring my love for him and asking him to help me live the full life that he had prepared for me.

I remember very little from my first eight years on earth, but I remember that night. I remember praying that modest prayer and feeling peace and joy wash over me. I remember bursting into tears of relief and excitement as weeks of questioning and uncertainty faded away, recognizing that I had finally found the answer. I knew then that heaven was to be my forever-home and that Jesus was my Saviour.

That one moment in my childhood is the most significant moment in my life, but it was only the beginning of the great adventure that God was to take me on. It was the first of many prayers of repentance, the first of many declarations of love, the first of many requests for guidance. For, just as it takes time and communication to build friendship with a new acquaintance, it takes time and communication to develop a relationship with God.

More than twenty years later, I have used just about every resource or suggestion I have received to support me in building my relationship with God. I have followed Bible reading plans, signed up for daily emails from world-renowned pastors and speakers, developed prayer lists, listened to podcasts, used online Bible study resources, read books and biographies, scheduled in quiet times with God morning, noon and night . . . the list goes on and on. And while all these things have been helpful and played their part in revealing more and more about God, I discovered that the way I best connect with him is to journal.

As a teenager, I was gifted my first journal from my brothers. I began by writing just a line or two about what each day had included: who I had seen, what I had done. Then slowly I introduced my feelings and responses to those daily events.

As the habit developed, I took more time to write down Bible verses or quotes that had impacted me in some way. I recorded my thoughts, my dreams, my worries and my reflections. I found that, by recording these things in my journal, it aided me in processing life's ups and downs, and helped me identify threads of God's faithfulness throughout my day-to-day living.

Over the last few years, I have developed the habit of writing out my prayers in full. Taking the time to thoughtfully articulate them has helped me to focus on what I am saying to God rather than getting distracted and allowing my mind to wander if I just pray silently in my head. By keeping a record of my prayers like this, I am better equipped to identify and celebrate the answers when they come. Similarly, while I am still waiting for answers, I can look back in my journal and be reassured that I have truly given the painful issues over to God and can trust him to act.

It took me many years to discover what works for me, and these same practices may not work for you. I do not know anyone who journals as much as I do, but I no longer compare myself to others or consider that to be a bad thing. The aim is to know God, not to simply match your daily habits to that of someone else. The challenge is to find what works for *you*. I am not an early morning person so I tend not to journal in the mornings, but I am intentional about setting aside time during the day—usually in the evening—to pray, read my Bible, and to journal all that God has revealed to me about himself that day. I'll often make notes in my phone of revelations or answered prayers as they happen, then record them in my journal later. I am easily distracted so I often choose quiet worship or instrumental music to play through headphones to block out all other noise and conversation. Sometimes it is necessary to journal inside but, whenever possible, I prefer to write outside. There, I feel my heart connect more easily to God, and I often hear him whisper back to me as I take in his beautiful creation.

I asked some friends how they best connect with God, and I was surprised at how varied the responses were:

> Connecting with God comes when I'm in the forest, working out to pop or rap music, and through worship. Another thing that has been happening recently is when I'm being hugged, I get revelation from the Lord then, too.

> Either outside seeing God's creation, in the car with my worship music on loud, or in a quiet space, just me and God. It depends on the day. If I can't hear God at all, I go and watch the waves. I'm guaranteed to find God in the sea.

I best connect with God through a special time of prayer, worship (belting out worship on a walk or in the car), and hearing about how God is speaking into someone else's life.

A certain chair in the kitchen, where I sometimes spend my devotional time . . . even in the shower—a quiet place where I'm alone is always good.

I find it best to connect with God when I'm sitting still in my room, listening to some music and journaling. Also after I exercise I feel that I can connect with God more, or water-colouring and making handmade Scripture cards.

One of my favourite ways is to go hillwalking, which I thoroughly enjoy . . . When I go with my friend, he is often a bit faster than me so there are long periods of time when we do not talk and these are valuable moments for me to focus on God and pray. As I soak up the awesomeness of his creation around me, it reminds me of how great God is. Being away from the distractions of home, books, etc, it helps me really put my mind to God and I usually spend wonderful quality time with God when I go hillwalking. And, strange as this may sound, sometimes towards the peak of the hill, when my legs start to give, or I start to cramp, that is when I pray even harder and it helps me to really focus on God's greatness and my weaknesses, and how God's greatness overcomes my weakness.

I set aside some time and sit down and get my Bible and journal out. I read through a passage, meditate on it and journal around it. Using the acronym S. O. A. P., I read through a Scripture (S), note down observations (O) from that Scripture, consider how to apply (A) it in my life, then pray (P) over what I have learnt.

The different environments described by these people illustrate how creative and personal God is. He considers our personality, our interests and our habits to reach out to us in unique ways. I think it's beautiful!

My relationship with God is unique to me, and so is the way I communicate with him. Now that I have discerned how I best connect with God, I am intentional about recreating that environment daily so that our conversation can continue and our relationship can grow.

Developing good habits is essential when getting to know God, but real joy is found when these good habits transition into relationship. The more you know God, the greater your love for him will grow, and the more time you will *want* to spend with him. But, first, we must learn to recognize his voice.

Samuel was a great prophet who served God throughout his lifetime. He was respected in Israel, sharing with the people wisdom and revelation from God, entering into intercessory prayer on the nation's behalf, and acting as judge and calling the rebellious nation to repentance. Perhaps most notably, however, Samuel anointed the first two kings of Israel: Saul and David. But before Samuel could step into his great God-ordained destiny, he first had to learn to commune with his Creator.

Samuel was born to a gracious, godly woman, Hannah, who wept and prayed for many years for a son of her own. She vowed that if God gave her a son, she would dedicate him to God for his lifetime. God looked down on her with compassion and, in due time, she became pregnant.

In the Bible, in 1 Samuel 1, we read that once Samuel was weaned, Hannah, true to her vow, presented her son to the priest, Eli, at the temple and Samuel served Eli there and learnt from him. One night, as Eli and Samuel lay down to sleep in the temple, Samuel heard someone call his name, so he ran through to where Eli was sleeping and said, "Here I am!" But Eli responded, "I did not call you, go back to sleep," and Samuel did so.

A second time, Samuel heard his name called and got up and went to check to see if Eli was all right. "Here I am," he said, "you called me." But once again, Eli told Samuel to return to bed.

As Samuel lay back down to sleep, he heard his name called a third time, so he ran to Eli's side. Then Eli realized that it was God who was calling the boy. Therefore, he instructed Samuel, "Lie back down, and if he calls you again, say to him, 'Speak, Lord, for your servant is listening.'" Samuel obeyed Eli and went back to his bed.

Once again, Samuel heard the Lord call his name, but this time he remained where he was and responded just as Eli had instructed: "Speak, Lord, I am listening." It took time, and instruction, and obedience, but Samuel soon learnt how to communicate with God. For all that God had planned for Samuel to fulfil on his behalf, it was absolutely vital that Samuel learnt to recognize the voice of God and to begin a conversation with the Almighty.

We may be in the habit of looking for God in the loud, demonstrative happenings around us; we may expect God's voice to follow trumpet calls or flashing lights. But God speaks, more often than not, in a quiet, tenacious whisper that may be missed if we do not still our hearts enough to listen for it.

There have been a couple of times in my life when I have been convinced that God has spoken a promise over my life when later, in hindsight, I realized I was greatly mistaken. You see, I paid too much attention to grand, emotional responses to a single encounter, then wasted much time weighing up pros and cons, trying to deliberate between God's voice and my own. But we can be assured that confusion and stress is not in God's character; on the contrary, those things are often evidences of our own involvement. I learnt that his promises are seldomly announced in one significant moment. Rather, God's voice is quietly persistent in providing clarity and leading us to our destiny. Therefore, if we truly want to know God for ourselves, we need to cultivate a peaceful mind and identify that place where we can be alone with God, quieten our own inner voice and tune in to his.

There are so many things around us to distract us from prayer: the constant chatter of media sources, your children arguing over the TV remote, honking horns and sirens from the street outside. But if journaling is not your thing, try something else. Some find declaring their prayers audibly not only drowns out the hum of white noise around them, but also ignites their own faith, finding power in hearing their declarations and requests spoken aloud. More creative individuals may find stillness amongst their art, whether painting, composing or movement.

It is not so important how one prays, but that we do so with an open heart and mind. Prayer is a conversation with God; it is two-way communication, not just a chance to update your holy wish list. Prayer creates an opportunity to connect with your Creator and to discover his heart for yourself! It requires honesty, vulnerability and trust. Tell him how you really feel: he can handle it. Ask him questions, share your doubts, express your concerns, then allow him a chance to *respond*. He's always listening. He's always ready to talk.

Or perhaps your challenge is not *how* to pray, but *where* to pray. My head and heart are most receptive to the voice of God when I am somewhere scenic, surrounded by nature: at the beach, up a hill, by the river, in a park, or, more conveniently, just sitting outside on my balcony. For you, it could be a specific room in your home, while you take the dog for a walk every morning, or a simple gesture, like a closed door, that alerts your family to your need for a moment alone. For Susanna Wesley, the mother of well-known hymn writer Charles Wesley (who penned over 6,000 hymns, including the Christmas favourite, "Hark! The Herald Angels Sing") and his eighteen siblings (yes, you read that right), a moment to herself was somewhat unheard of. However, in the midst of chaos in their home, her children knew that whenever they saw their mother throw her apron over her head, she was not to be disturbed, for that was when she would be speaking to her Lord. She understood that finding the right location for prayer is less about identifying a physical space, and more about creating a mental space: a moment to pause and to remove all other distractions so that you can focus solely on God.

As we begin our adventure, we should also be intentional about cultivating a thankful heart. Prayer is not just about presenting our requests to God; it is an opportunity to thank him for all the good things that he gives us. We all have something that we are grateful for: our life, our health, our relationships, our home, our job, our education. You may not feel very grateful for some of these things at this present point in time, but pick one and begin by thanking God for his provision in that area of your life. Rather than focusing on what has not turned out quite as expected, we can tend our hearts by showing gratitude for the small victories so far and by trusting that God has an even better plan still to come. He loves us so much that he is not so preoccupied with giving us what we want now, but shaping us into people who will embrace the adventure that he still wants to take us on.

If a child asks his father to buy him a chocolate bar every time they are in the supermarket together, it is likely that the father will often say no. There may be times that the father grants the boy's wish but the father knows that too much chocolate for a young boy is bad for his health. The boy, on the other hand, does not care about his weight, his waistline or his oral health; he is only aware that his request has been denied.

But parents make decisions based on what is best for their child in the long run, don't they? We want our children to learn to make healthy choices, to grasp the lesson of delaying gratification, or to understand how to deal with disappointment. We do not adhere to a child's every request because we see and understand the greater objective of guiding them into maturity. And God does the same for us. His answers to our prayers are not always what we want to hear, or even understand, but he does it for our long-term benefit. We only see what is right in front of us, but God sees far beyond the snippet of time that we behold, therefore we can trust his eternal perspective.

It is often not until months or even years later that we see God's hand in the detail of our lives, especially through periods of pain and difficulty. Sometimes we never understand why something happened the way it did. But what we can be certain of is that God is faithful, even when we are not. You may not yet have a personal relationship with him, but I can assure you that he has had his hand on your life from the beginning. He has loved you, protected you and guided you, even if you have been entirely unaware of it until now.

The most important gift we receive from God when we enter into a relationship with him is his Spirit. The Holy Spirit enables us to communicate with God, helping us to speak when words fail us, and to discern his voice when he answers. It is God's Spirit that makes the words of the Bible come alive and become active within us; he brings revelation and meaning to passages written thousands of years ago. His presence empowers us to do that which seems impossible to do alone, and he acts like an internal navigation system when following God's purpose for our lives. It is impossible to live the adventure God has prepared for us without the help of the Holy Spirit.

Perhaps you are beginning to feel a bit overwhelmed by all this. How can we really know God personally? How can we possibly endeavour to live the life that he has planned for us? How do we figure out what that is? What if we mess up? But God is a gracious God. He gives us free choice to live the way we want to live. Yet when what we want is to live the life that he has planned for us—a life full of faith, surprises, miracles and adventure—he will not let us miss it. When we truly seek his purpose for our lives, he *will* show us the way. He does not leave us stuck and confused, trying to ascertain his plans. Even when we wander off course, or take matters into our own hands, when we surrender to him again, he will always meet us where we are and gently steer us back onto the right path. God is just waiting for us to invite him to take us on the adventure of a lifetime.

When we surrender our lives to God and allow him to direct our steps, we also open up a whole host of new possibilities. God does not need our ability—he is able to do all things (Matthew 19:26)—but he loves it when we make ourselves *available* to him, to be directed and used as part of his great plan. When we make our hands and feet available to God, he can and will do far more with them than we could ever do ourselves. If we surrender the direction and purpose of our lives to him, he can take us on the greatest adventure: one we would never dream of embarking on alone. Life with God becomes a partnership; God uses us to achieve his purposes, and we have the opportunity and privilege to be a part of something far greater than ourselves, something we could not enter into without him.

When we first embark on an adventure with God, it rarely resembles adventure. More often than not, it begins with small, hidden acts of obedience that appear insignificant in human eyes. Indeed, some of life's greatest opportunities can be found masked behind such trivial tasks. But nothing is insignificant in the eyes of God, and, when we prove ourselves to be obedient with the small things, God will entrust us with much more.

Your adventure can begin today. Start with what you know: show kindness, be generous, practise patience. Ask God to help you see a need and let him show you how you can help meet that need. As we begin to live in a way that reflects God's plan for humankind, as he describes in his Word, he will open our eyes to more opportunities where our specific skillset can be used to make a difference. God can only use what we are willing to share, so take a look at what he has already blessed you with and start there. You will soon be amazed at what God orchestrates around you: the conversations you have, the people you meet, the exciting ways in which you get to serve and the joy you experience living every moment with God by your side.

The closer we draw towards God, the more we see him at work in our lives. Our problems and worries diminish as our view of God expands. When we begin to see life from God's perspective, the opinions of others will matter less because we accept that we are part of something much greater than what is evident to the naked eye. As we spend time with God, our hearts and minds are renewed and our desires and dreams align with his. Disappointments are no longer so disappointing, because we trust that he gives (and takes away) for the sake of the greater good. When we draw close to God, we find in him not only a Father, but a teacher, a master, a friend. He knows us better than we know ourselves and takes delight in satisfying the deepest desires of our heart.

Corrie ten Boom, a Dutch watchmaker who was imprisoned for helping Jews escape during the Nazi Holocaust in World War Two, is supposed to have said: "Never be afraid to trust an unknown future to a known God." It can be scary to face uncertainty and we feel helpless when we do not know what will happen next, but when we first get to know God, the future becomes a well of endless possibilities. The more we *know* him, the easier it is to *trust* him.

Today, God declares good things over you. He loves you and desires to heal your hurts, contradict your insecurities, and remind you of who he created you to be. He wants to enter into a conversation with you, but he awaits your invitation. Start today. Find a quiet place, open your heart to him, and begin.

3
Designed for Adventure

When I was growing up, my family and I attended a small, conservative church not far from our home. It was a community of warm, generous people who loved God and diligently taught his Word. There, I built a firm foundation of biblical knowledge and had the privilege of being mentored and invested in by the older generations. It was there, too, that I had the opportunity to begin to serve and help out at the weekly Kids' Club while barely more than a kid myself.

But as I moved through my teenage years, I sought to widen my friendship pool and to broaden my opportunities and responsibilities within the church body, so I began visiting a larger, neighbouring church and their youth group on occasion too. During one such visit, I happened to notice a poster for an up-coming worship event at the local conference arena and, without thinking much of it, I popped the date into my diary.

The worship initiative, called *Souled Out*, was to be a pilot and the first of four similar events to be held throughout the year; it was a new venture led by two men in their mid-twenties seeking to unite churches from across the city and across denominations in worship. I attended all four events that year, always excitedly anticipating the arrival of the next.

The following year, as attendance at *Souled Out* events continued to grow and the team behind it began to press into what God was doing through them and their obedience to the vision he had given them, more help was needed. I eagerly signed up. I was to be part of the stewarding team and take responsibility for showing people to their seats and assisting with any further help required by members of the public. I absolutely *loved* being involved.

I served on the stewarding team for the first three events that second year and by the time the fourth event rolled round, I had been asked to step in as the Stewarding Team Leader. Oh boy, was I thrilled! Yes, please! The funny thing about me is that I crave responsibility. I love the challenge it brings, I thrive under pressure, and cherish the rewarding sense of achievement when it is all done. Leading the Stewarding Team was the opportunity I had been waiting for.

The year after, I remained as the Stewarding Team Leader, gradually taking on more and more responsibility. From there I was asked to join the *Souled Out* Organizing Team and delegated the Stewarding Team responsibilities to another volunteer to allow me to adopt the role of Event Manager. Oh, and did I mention I was just nineteen years old?

You see, I didn't set out with the end goal of overseeing worship events attended by over 1,000 people; I simply wanted to be a part of it and serve in some way. But through time, willingness and obedience, God opened up new opportunities for me to step into and to grow into. It was through my involvement in *Souled Out* that I identified that I had the gift of administration. I may have known I was organized, but my gift did not present itself until it had had the opportunity to be exercised. That team saw potential in me, took a risk on me and, unknowingly, catapulted me further into my adventure.

Through my experience with *Souled Out*, I became known to church leaders across the city, and this would later lead me into a pioneering staff role in a local church. But more on that later.

So how do we go about identifying the gifts God has birthed in us? Where do we start? It is easier for some than for others, but my best advice would be to just serve. Get plugged into a local church and give it a go. "Give what a go?" you ask. Anything! Anything that takes your fancy. If the nursery team are short of helpers, offer to help them out. If you find that spending an hour with babies crying and toddlers tugging at your leg is not your thing, then graciously bow out and give something else a go. Can you make yourself a cup of coffee? Then why not begin to do it for others? If you find that you are too busy chatting to the first person that you served and the line is backing up, perhaps you are more gifted with people and can begin to explore opportunities to welcome and connect with visitors in the church. If you manage to serve a hundred cups of coffee, wipe the tables, empty the bin and restock the sugar sachets all before the kettle has finished boiling, then perhaps you have an eye for detail, and help or administration is part of your gifting.

The bottom line is to just grasp an opportunity and give it a go. If you feel uneasy or worried about inadvertently joining a team you did not wish to, why not speak to the team leader beforehand and ask them for the chance to serve for a couple of weeks before you commit to anything? Believe me, most team leaders will jump at the chance to add people to their team and, if it does not seem like a good fit for you, it will probably not feel like a good fit for the team leader either, and they will happily let you bow out and bless you as you move on to something else.

But how will you know when you have identified your gift? Well, there are a number of different questions you can ask yourself:

- **What do you enjoy doing?** My friends used to (and sometimes still do) laugh at how excited I get about plans, files, lists and colour-coded spreadsheets. It is not the items themselves that I get excited about, but the countless hours of consideration, preparation and precious information that they represent. These stationery items are evidence of my gift in action, and that is what excites me.
- **What frustrates you?** Believe it or not, this too can point you towards your gift. Often, when you are gifted in a particular way, you look at certain aspects of church (or work or home life) and get frustrated by the lack in those areas. Perhaps you get frustrated by what is being done and you are inspired with new methods to improve. Now, hear me, this is not permission for you to *complain*. Complaining about something only points out the faults. Inspired ideas, however, seek to provide improved *solutions*. Have you considered that, in fact, you may be the solution to some of the problems that you see? These moments may also help point you towards your gift.
- **What do you do well?** Sometimes we make things difficult for ourselves, and complicate matters which are plain and simple. So, what are you good at? What do others say you do well? Others will see the gift in you too, sometimes even before you do. Ask your team leader, your boss, your colleagues and your friends

what you do well, and what you perhaps do not do quite so well (and be prepared for honest answers). There is a reason God made you with specific gifts and skills; it is not luck or a coincidence that you enjoy and thrive in what you do well. This is all part of God's careful design for your life, in preparation for the purpose he has for you.

- **What can you not stop talking about?** I did not notice it myself, but when I was involved with *Souled Out*, I (unintentionally) introduced the topic into *every* conversation, no matter who I was with. It was such a huge part of my life, and I was incredibly passionate about it, that I just could not help but talk about it every chance I got! Recognizing this highlighted for me how important my involvement in *Souled Out* was. It played a small yet significant part in God's big purpose for my life, and he used it to identify and develop gifts in me. It set me on a path that would lead to even greater and more rewarding opportunities in the future.

We know that our bodies have many different parts to them: limbs, organs, bones, tissue, muscles . . . the list is a long one. And we also know that each part, no matter how big or small, seen or unseen, has an important and unique purpose. We each have a mouth so that we can talk, eat and kiss. We have lungs so that we can breathe and extract the vital oxygen we need from the air around us. And the tiny hairs all over our body, often entirely forgotten about, play an essential part in helping to regulate our body temperature. The Bible uses the illustration of a body to describe the global Church: that is, the collection of every individual on earth who has accepted salvation from their sins through Jesus Christ and entered into a relationship with God.

In 1 Corinthians 12, we are reminded that God has arranged every single member in the body carefully and intentionally. There is a reason that we are all different because no body is made up of only one part. Can you imagine a body of eyes? We could see everything going on around us, but have no hands or feet to take action. Or a body made only of mouths? We would have plenty to say but lack the ability to listen. Therefore, we all have different skills, different gifts, different purposes so that we work in collaboration with the other members of the global Church and, *together*, operate effectively.

I would encourage you to read for yourself more about the different gifts given by God and enabled by the Holy Spirit, as described in various passages in the Bible. But to help get you started, I have listed the main Bible passages with the gifts catalogued in them below.

Just before the body analogy, 1 Corinthians 12 provides a list of gifts given to the global Church through her members. They are:

- wisdom
- knowledge
- faith
- discernment
- apostolic leadership
- prophecy
- teaching
- miracles
- healing
- helping
- administration
- speaking in tongues
- interpretation of tongues.

In Romans 12, the Apostle Paul explains that each of us who have received salvation through Jesus Christ have also received a different gift according to the grace given to us, and urges us to use them. The gifts he lists are:

- prophecy
- service
- teaching
- encouragement
- generosity
- leadership
- mercy.

Ephesians 4 also mentions some of the gifts God gives us, to equip us for ministry and to strengthen the global Church. They include:

- apostolic leadership
- prophecy
- evangelism
- pastoral care
- teaching.

God chooses to give us the gifts that will serve us best in the vision and purposes that he has prepared for us; it is all part of a much grander plan. But there will be times in life when it is necessary and important to serve other people's visions and passions first. I do not believe that God will trust us with a vision of our own until we have proved that we can be trusted to uphold someone else's. I have served and supported many other visions in my lifetime; this was easy when it aligned with my own, but proved somewhat more challenging when, at times, I might have chosen to do things a little differently. In those moments, I found that these passionate visionaries grew frustrated by my lack of passion for their particular dream or area of service.

I used to think that I was lacking something, that I was not spiritual enough to see the need or, indeed, that the world had deadened me to the spiritually lost in those communities, those cities, that demographic. It was not until much later that I began to recognize that God gives different people different passions (and gifts) to ensure that *all* his work gets done, and not just in one area (geographical or otherwise). If the whole church body was passionate about and gifted at leading worship, we would do well at praising God and be led into spiritual connection with him, but have no-one to explain the Scriptures to us. If your entire church congregation was passionate about reaching the elderly, a lot of broken people would make a whole lot of mistakes in life before they had the opportunity to learn about Jesus.

But we are part of a *body* and we all have different functions and different parts to play. The key for us is to find our unique role to play and then to play it *well*. It is all part of the journey to identify not only your gifts, but also the passions within which they can be used. I now recognize that it is important that my passions are different to those of my leaders, my peers and my friends, because there is a whole world of work still to be done in God's kingdom! We cannot all prioritize a tiny corner of the plan but, rather, we must be equipped and released into that which God has called us to. I have had to initiate some difficult conversations with pastors, leaders, family members and friends over the years because I have recognized that God's priority for my life in that season was no longer within a ministry I had previously served in and, after prayerful consideration, it was time to step back from a role or responsibility. Though good in and of themselves, they were no longer the *best* use of my gifts and my time.

As I mentioned earlier, my involvement with *Souled Out* later opened up an incredible opportunity for me to work for my local church. The role was a dream come true for me, and the experience and leadership I received there was truly defining. I will be forever grateful for the risk they took employing me: a naive twenty-three-year-old. The trust they placed in me to carry such responsibility, and the time they invested in me, not just to benefit my work, but to shape my character and develop me spiritually too, was invaluable.

However, during my time working there, I struggled with many insecurities. I often felt that my work was not making much difference. My role kept me, for the most part, behind a desk, sat at a computer, or in meetings with other church leaders. I longed to be on the "front line" of ministry—on the streets, helping the broken, showing God's love in more practical ways—not because I was necessarily good at it, but because I imagined that that was where the "real" work was.

As I privately struggled with these thoughts, I was approached by a group within the church who had pioneered an outreach ministry in their neighbourhood. They envisioned holding a summer fun day for their community, while incorporating personal testimonies and the gospel message into the programme. And they needed my help.

We formed a small group that took the lead on planning for and executing the event; we all brought very different gifts and skills to the table, and this proved both helpful and challenging at times. You see, as an administrator, my priority was to ensure that every document, spreadsheet, application form and risk assessment was properly and carefully completed, while those with the gift of faith, for example, struggled to see why it was so important that I had every "i" dotted and every "t" crossed, because they trusted the Holy Spirit to intervene and act on our behalf. My focus was to ensure that the barbeque food was prepared according to health and safety guidelines, while those with the gift of evangelism were more interested in identifying the right people to share their personal journey of faith.

The process to make this dream a reality for our small organizing team was not an easy one. Our priorities and processes clashed regularly, and we had to navigate many misunderstandings. But as time went on, we began to realize that none of us were invalidated in our priorities or agendas just because they were different. It was exactly for this reason that we were the right individuals to be compiled in this group: because we were all *different*. It was necessary that our gifts and skills and perspectives were vastly contrasted because the event would never have happened if we had had only some gifts without the others.

By the end of that summer, I had learnt that we should all be demonstrating God's love in the opportunities and circumstances we find ourselves in, but we, the body of Christ, operate *best* when we operate in our own God-attributed gifts. I took the opportunity to walk the streets in that same community to connect with people and to invite them to the event, but my focus, my *priority*, was to use the gifts that God had given me to work behind the scenes and to operate in my *strengths*. By using that particular event as an illustration, God helped me see that my employment (as well as my voluntary service) was key to the work that he was doing in and through my local church.

However, we should also be careful not to be too limited by our gifts either. Sometimes it is good to operate in other areas that perhaps pose greater challenge or anxiety. I felt far from comfortable knocking on doors and inviting people in that community to the summer fun day, but I knew that the only way in which I could grow and overcome my fear was by stepping out of my comfort zone.

We are reminded in 1 Corinthians 12 that it is God who selects and gives these different gifts to us, as he chooses: "Now there are varieties of gifts, but the same Spirit; and there are varieties of service, but the same Lord; and there are varieties of activities, but it is the same God who empowers them all in everyone" (1 Corinthians 12:4–6). We cannot look upon another and wish we had their gift because, in so doing, we are rejecting the good gifts that God has given to us. When we each fully live in our own gifting and calling, there is no need for envy to creep into our thoughts because we are fulfilling the unique calling that was specially chosen by God himself, just for us. Our gift, our passion, our calling has the heavenly seal of approval. No-one can steal that from you; only you can deny the purpose that the Father has placed on you if you allow jealousy, or fear, or busyness to rob you of it.

Resist the temptation to try to do everything and spread yourself too thinly—for some this is easy, for others (like me) much less so—but be assured that sometimes it is OK to say no. It is far more profitable for you and your church if you focus on serving in areas that you are skilled and gifted in, and allow "gaps" to be filled by other individuals within the church. By filling a role that is not ours to fill, we steal away the opportunity for others to identify and develop their own gifts. Instead, serve in a way that is most spiritually fruitful.

There is also a danger in allowing the busyness of life to deter us from serving in our local church. I served in *Souled Out* through four years of studying for my Bachelor of Science degree in Physics and Education at university and I never missed an event. Many of my peers would step back during exam times or when deadlines were looming, but I firmly believe that when we work hard, do our best and then leave it in God's hands, he blesses us abundantly. Countless times God moved deadlines, cancelled lectures and postponed exams to allow me to give myself fully to both my studies and to my ministry service.

Perhaps you have already successfully identified your gifts and are privileged to be leading a team or ministry operating in those skills. As leaders, we are called to disciple and equip others as they journey through their Christian walk. But one of our biggest challenges is to release those people when they are ready to pursue all that God has called them to. If they are heavily involved in serving in church, it can be very difficult to allow them to walk away. If you have come to depend on them, it can be a challenge to find someone else to fill their shoes. But instead of dwelling on what you (personally) are losing, choose to focus on what the global

Church is gaining and celebrate the part you played in God's call on that individual's life.

Leaders must resist getting frustrated at the lack of passion and interest others have in their ministry, and instead use it to gauge how suitable an individual is to their cause. We should encourage people to chase after the passion God has given them, for in it most likely lies their God-appointed purpose.

We rarely need to go looking for our purpose: purpose finds us. It is that thing that plagues your thoughts when you are trying to sleep at night. Or the cause that penetrates your daydreams. It provokes passion, excitement and a righteous anger to rise up within you. And when an opportunity presents itself for you to enter into the battle, a fire burns in your soul like you have never experienced before.

Michael Apted's movie *Amazing Grace* features the life and works of William Wilberforce, an English politician who led the movement to abolish the slave trade in the late eighteenth and early nineteenth centuries. Following his conversion to evangelical Christianity in 1785, Wilberforce toyed with the notion of leaving politics and a life in the public eye. He sought counsel from friends, including Prime Minister William Pitt, and Anglican clergyman John Newton, a former slave ship captain, best known for penning the hymn that the movie is named after. In response to his dilemma, their on-screen counterparts state, "Mr Wilberforce, we understand you are having problems choosing whether to do the work of God, or the work of a political activist. We humbly suggest that you can do both."[4]

Wilberforce was an intelligent man with great passion and focus, but he was torn between living for God and living for justice. It took some time, plus the insight of his friends (friends are great at bringing fresh perspective, are they not?) to realize that his privileged responsibility within parliament positioned him perfectly to carry out the unique role God had created him for. He did not have to choose one cause or the other: they complemented one another perfectly.

How God created you and where he has placed you is in exact keeping with how he will use you. Yes, he might call you into full-time ministry, but more often than not, he is calling you to bring his light into your workplace, your college, your school, your family, your friendship group or your neighbourhood. He uses the skills and gifts that he has created you with to open doors of opportunity for you to serve him and to build his kingdom. We need to own who he has created us to be, because, if we do not rise up to take our place in this world, we can be sure that the enemy will claim it.

You may look around and think to yourself, "Why has someone not done anything about that?" But is it possible that, in fact, *you* are that someone? The world needs people who are ready to stand up and say, "This is my time. This is my opportunity." The Bible tells us of a young woman who did just that.

In the book of Esther, King Ahasuerus held a feast for all his kingdom officials and commanded his queen, Vashti, to join them so he could show off her beauty. But upon her refusal, she lost her crown and the king's aides suggested that virgins be presented to the king so that he could inspect them and select a new queen.

At that same time, a Jew called Mordecai was living in Susa, a Benjaminite whose people had been taken from Jerusalem by King Nebuchadnezzar of Babylon 117 years earlier. He had raised Hadassah, better known as Esther, his cousin, since her childhood, for her father and mother had died.

Esther was very beautiful and was brought into the palace to join the king's harem with other virgins from the kingdom. However, Mordecai warned her not to make known to the palace her Jewish heritage. Having then been subjected to twelve months of preparation, as was the custom, Esther and the rest of the harem were presented, one by one, to the king. When the king met Esther, she instantly won grace and favour in his sight, more than any of the other women he had already seen, so he duly crowned her his new queen.

Some time later, the king promoted a man called Haman to lead all the palace officials, and the people dutifully bowed down to their new leader and worshipped him. However, Mordecai the Jew did not; he would bow to no-one but the one, true God. This made Haman so furious that he set about plotting to destroy not just Mordecai but all the Jews in the kingdom.

Haman was devious and presented to the king a decree to kill all the Jews throughout the kingdom and successfully tricked the king into making it official with his royal seal, arguing that the Jewish subjects did not observe the king's laws. When Mordecai and the people of Susa heard about the decree, they tore their clothes, donned sackcloth and ashes, as was the custom in the day during a period of mourning, and cried bitterly throughout the city.

I want to pause here for a moment, because what strikes me most in this part of the story is the emotional response displayed by the Jews when their authorities discriminated against them. "Well of course they are upset," you might be thinking, "they have been sentenced to death!" But do *we* not also witness laws and decrees being passed in our world today that discriminate against nationality, race, gender, faith, beliefs? We watch our generation turn their backs on God, but a passive-aggressive post on social media is near the extent that most of us will rise to. Why are we not moved to tears and mourning as our world rejects its Saviour? Why have so many of us become immune to the injustice and persecution of God's people all over the world? We need to start taking these things *personally*.

When Esther discovered what had happened, the queen was seized by fear, as she herself was also a Jew. She sent clothes to Mordecai to encourage him to remove the sackcloth he was wearing, but he did not accept them. Instead, Mordecai sent a copy of the decree to Esther and urged her to speak to the king to plead for the lives of her people.

This request, however, only increased the fear in Esther's heart, for she knew that unless the king summoned someone to himself, any who approached him were sure to be put to death, unless the king held out his royal sceptre to them and spared their life. Esther had not been summoned to the king for over a month.

Then Mordecai spoke the words we all associate best with the biblical account of Esther's life: "Do not think to yourself that in the king's palace you will escape any more than all the other Jews. For if you keep silent at this time, relief and deliverance will rise for the Jews from another place, but you and your father's house will perish. And who knows whether you have not come to the kingdom for such a time as this?" (Esther 4:13–14).

For such a time as this.

Esther had been obedient to her cousin Mordecai when he had suggested she present herself to join the king's harem. Her beauty had won her the king's affection and the crown. Oblivious to the special role God had for her to fulfil, she was faithful with what was available to her. But we can see that God had strategically placed her there to save his beloved Jewish people. Was she ready to step up to the plate? Was she willing to accept the role that she was created for, a role that no-one but she could fill?

Esther responded to Mordecai once more, asking him to gather all the Jews in Susa and to fast on her behalf, and informing him that she and her maids would do the same. Then on the third day she would approach the king in the name of her people, "and if I perish, I perish" (Esther 4:16b).

She stepped up to the plate. She stepped forward, knowing it may even mean her end. She stepped up for the greater good, to save a nation from injustice and persecution. And God used her mightily in his great plan for his people. We know about her story because she was faithful with what she had been given and what was made available to her. She has a whole book of the Bible named after her, because she accepted the unique role that God had created her for.

Every experience that Esther had faced until that moment—both the good and the bad—had prepared her and positioned her for success. God knew that this moment would come so he had used her faith, her painful family history and her loyalty to her cousin to make sure that she was ready. That didn't make it easy, or comfortable, for her to approach the king uninvited—she still required courage to do what was being asked of her—but her obedience saved an entire nation from death. How's that for purpose? Her adventure led her to the palace, right into the royal family, and perfectly positioned her for all that God had called her to do.

Voices all around us will constantly try to label us, influence us and put us in neat little boxes: the media, our bosses and teachers, politicians and professionals. The only way to combat that is to draw close to the One who created us and ask him who he has made us to be. None of us were created to fit neatly into categories or boxes because we were all made to be different. There is only one of you! Find your own sphere of influence and represent Jesus well in that place.

When we give power to the voices around us, sometimes even well-meaning ones, confusion and stress begin to impress upon us. We become so distracted trying to meet the expectations of others that we forget to listen out for the voice of God. But now is the time to press into the future that God is calling us to. We need to be brave, like Esther, and step into our destiny. We were created, positioned and called, for such a time as this.

The gifts and passions within us hold the potential for all that God wants to do on earth in the next one hundred years. Our response will determine how much of that potential becomes reality.

4
Essential Tools for the Journey

In J. R. R. Tolkien's novel *The Hobbit* we follow the journey of Bilbo Baggins, a small, unassuming fellow who enjoys his home comforts and relishes his food. He lives a quiet life of routine and respect until the wizened wizard Gandalf comes knocking on his door and invites him on an adventure.

Gandalf had been tasked to find the fourteenth member of a dwarf assembly, endeavouring to win back their home under the Lonely Mountain, and he believes Bilbo is the right man for the job. On meeting the hobbit for the first time, the company of dwarves are doubtful that he is up to the task, and Bilbo begins to doubt himself too. In Peter Jackson's movie adaptation, the old wizard rises from his chair and responds, "There is a lot more to him than appearances suggest, and he's got a lot more to offer than any of you know . . . including himself. You must trust me on this."[5]

The following morning, Bilbo wakes up to find the company of dwarves gone. He is still unsure that he really has what it takes, or if he truly desires to swap his cosy abode for risk, uncertainty and challenge. But, after only a moment's hesitation, he grabs his bag and is seen darting through the village to catch up with the group.

"Here, Mr Bilbo, where are you off to?" calls his neighbour.

"Can't stop, I'm already late," Bilbo pants in response.

"Late for what?" enquires the other hobbit.

"I'm going on an adventure!"

Having then caught up with the group, Bilbo is given a pony to ease the physical strain of the quest. Unbeknownst to the others, he is allergic to horsehair and immediately begins to sneeze. Patting down his pockets, he shouts, "Stop! We have to turn around! I've forgotten my handkerchief."

"You'll have to manage without pocket handkerchiefs, and a good many other things, Bilbo Baggins, before we reach your journey's end," Gandalf assures him. "You were born to the rolling hills and little rivers of the Shire, but home is now behind you, the world is ahead."

From the beginning of this tale, Bilbo is intrigued by the idea of going on an adventure, but reason causes him to hesitate on more than one occasion. Gandalf chose him for a purpose, but he doubts himself and feels poorly prepared for the journey ahead.

I think we can feel like this at times too; God calls us to join his quest, but sometimes we are excited by the *idea* more than the reality. We hesitate and deliberate over whether or not we will respond positively. And more often than not, we feel ill-equipped for all that we anticipate ahead of us.

It's ironic that we often seek to hurry God along and leap into opportunities that we are not ready for, yet worry about our preparedness when he asks us to step into a new season. Yet God is a loving God, and he knows us better than we know ourselves. He knows what we will face, and whether or not we are ready to face it. That is not to say we will always feel ready ourselves, but he looks into the depths of our hearts and recognizes when our faith, our trust, our courage is ready to carry us into the next season.

Perhaps, like Bilbo, we get caught up in worrying about leaving behind home comforts when really our focus should be our emotional and spiritual preparation. We cannot map out each step that we will take on our journey, or save for the needs we will face along the way, but we can work on developing our character and spiritual disciplines. Then, no matter when God calls, where he calls us to or what he calls us to, we will be ready to respond in faith to whatever challenges lie ahead.

In this chapter, we will explore some lessons and habits that will better equip us for our adventure.

Be devoted

In Acts 2 we read about the very first Christians. Jesus had ascended back into heaven, having completed his work on earth following his resurrection, and he had left the disciples alone, tasked with telling the world about him. Talk about a challenge! Yet they succeeded, didn't they? The fame of Jesus has spread, spanning countries and generations and we still share testimonies of his power today.

However, the disciples were no longer under the watchful eye of their Saviour, their teacher, their Lord. What if they had let fear, or pride or doubt stop them from entering into their next season without Jesus standing next to them? Then where would we all be?

The key is this: they were devoted *all by themselves* (Acts 2:42). Jesus had spent three years with them, teaching them about God's love, demonstrating the right way to live, and using miraculous events and parables to illustrate his mercy and love. He had equipped them with firsthand experiences of the kindness and justice he had shown to the world; he now also empowered them with the gift of the Holy Spirit, anointing them with boldness, and the ability to speak in languages they had not learnt so that the gospel could spread beyond their own, limited means.

Yet, if these first Christians had been satisfied with their existing knowledge of God, they would not have grown or journeyed any further. Our past experiences of God are important, but they merely provide us with a foundation upon which we must continue to build. It is our responsibility to continually press into him and seek a fresh revelation of him every day if we are to continue growing and working out his call on our lives. We cannot depend on yesterday's faith for what God wants to do in our lives tomorrow.

At the end of 2013, I sensed that God wanted to do something new in me, but I was coasting along in my life and in my faith, and somehow expected to coast right into God's new season for me. But that is not how God works. I was not ready for the new season and the longer I coasted, the longer I delayed the opportunity to enter into that new season.

In my journal, I penned these words:

The thing is, no resolution or next step will come if I'm not seeking it. I've all but neglected my prayer and Bible-reading habits (limited as they were anyway) and have been distracted by TV and movies. I need to once again establish daily habits (stronger this time) and begin bettering myself and my relationship with God otherwise I'll continue to coast along, losing out or delaying God's plans for me in work, in life and in relationships.

Our daily habits may ebb and flow as we journey through different seasons of life, but our devotion to God must be resolute if we wish to fully enter into the adventure he has laid out before us. It took me many more months to establish effective habits, but the real change was brought about when I began to pursue God to truly know him, and not just because it was "the right thing to do".

I realized that I had wasted too much time treating my Bible reading and prayer time like items on my daily checklist. We form habits to ensure that priorities remain so, but as we begin to see the fruit of our devotion, our habits develop into acts of intimacy. As our love for God grows and we experience true joy in his presence, we will instinctively become devoted all by ourselves.

This means that we cannot depend on the faith of our pastor, our spouse, our mentor, our home group leader, or anyone else around us, but that we take responsibility for our relationship with God and invest time and effort in pursuing him and knowing him intimately.

Matthew 6:33 encourages us to first and most importantly seek God's kingdom and his righteousness (his way of doing and being right—the attitude and character of God), and all other things will be given to us also. As we fix our eyes and attention on God, everything else—our fears, our hopes, our sin, our desires—resolve themselves as a beautiful by-product of God's work in our lives. The more we open our hearts to him, the more freedom he has to straighten out our crooked desires and to illuminate the dark corners of our hearts with his glorious light.

And as we fully devote ourselves to the Father, our hearts and minds are changed by the Holy Spirit who is at work in us. We become more like Christ, because the fruit of that same Spirit is love, joy, peace, patience, kindness, goodness, faithfulness, gentleness, self-control (Galatians 5:22–3).

Being devoted all by ourselves is the key to equipping ourselves for our next season; it unlocks every other tool we will need for the journey.

Work from rest

None of us like to feel anxious but it is increasingly becoming the accepted norm in today's culture. Stress, worry, busyness: they are part of everyday life. I can recall feeling, in my early twenties, that these things were something to strive for, and that I was not fulfilling my call to serve in the local church if I failed to fill every evening of the week with church activities. In fact, I had a sense of achievement and pride when my week was fully booked.

But filling our weeks with vigorous church activity is not what God asks of us. In fact, it may be quite the opposite. Around that same time in my life, I read a quote that would remain a constant challenge every day since: "If the devil can't make you bad, he'll make you busy" (attributed to Corrie ten Boom). Ouch. And it is true. The majority of the spiritually dry periods in my life have not been a result of sin, but a result of too much church activity and not enough rest at the feet of the One I serve.

The Bible tells the story of two sisters, Mary and Martha. These women, along with their brother Lazarus, were good friends of Jesus and they appear in the Gospel narrative a number of times. On one occasion, Jesus visited their village, and Martha invited him into their house for tea.

While her sister Mary sat at Jesus' feet, listening to his teaching, Martha busied herself serving everyone with food and drink, ensuring everyone was comfortable and satisfied. She shot disapproving looks at her sister, frustrated that she had been left to do the work herself, until finally she implored, "Lord, do you not care that my sister has left me to serve alone? Tell her then to help me." But the Lord answered her, "Martha, Martha, you are anxious and troubled about many things, but one thing is necessary. Mary has chosen the good portion, which will not be taken away from her" (Luke 10:40b–2).

I know this story so well. For years I had always related to Martha and could not understand why she was reprimanded like this. Surely being hospitable and showing kindness was also considered obedience to Jesus' teaching? But what Jesus was saying was, unless we find our rest in God, no amount of feverish activity or serving, even in the greatest ministries, will achieve very much. We must remain rooted in the Life-Giver.

I am no gardener, but I have attempted to keep a few house plants over the years. We all know that plants need the very basics: water and sunlight. They also require the correct soil and will occasionally need repotting as they grow. But the only way we can encourage a plant to flower or produce fruit is if it remains firmly attached to its roots.

In John 15, Jesus uses the analogy of a vine to explain to his disciples just how important it is to remain in good relationship with him. He is the vine and we are the branches, therefore we will remain spiritually healthy only when we stay connected to him, because through him is supplied that which we need to live. When we are rooted in him, our lives will produce evidence of that through the joy we carry and the spiritual fruit we bear. It is the vine's responsibility to provide everything needed to sustain life and channel it into the branches; the branches depend on the vine and produce fruit almost effortlessly when in a healthy state.

You may know, also, that healthy shrubs must be pruned from time to time. These plants are not pruned because there is something wrong with them, but because the gardener recognizes the potential in them and wants to encourage them to flourish. Similarly, it is when we face trials and difficulties that our faith is stretched and we learn to be more dependent on God. In these seasons, we grow even more, become stronger and are enabled to produce even more fruit.

On the other hand, when we do not root ourselves in Christ, we quickly become unhealthy; we cut ourselves off from the Life-source, we dry out and we fail to produce good fruit. We try to go it alone but end up so focused on remaining healthy ourselves that we have no energy left to be fruitful. I've been there: feeling physically, emotionally and spiritually drained, beginning to resent the ministry you are serving in, allowing attitudes and priorities to slip. It is a terrible place to be.

When we find our rest in Christ, our serving becomes infinitely easier. We not only find it easier to identify where best to serve, we also become more effective in our serving because we are fuelled by Christ himself, and not our own feeble efforts.

True rest equips us to fight the schemes of the enemy. I believe it was Elisabeth Elliot who once wrote: "Rest is a weapon given to us by God. The enemy hates it because he wants you stressed and occupied." Considering rest as a weapon almost seems counterintuitive, but God's ways are rarely understood. Waging war against the enemy from a state of rest allows God to fight for us, rather than us entering into the battle depending on our own efforts where we don't stand a chance. In those instances, when we are stressed and occupied, we are deaf to God's reassuring voice and blind to his guiding hand.

We must prioritize true spiritual rest (not laziness!) and be careful not to get so caught up in frantic activity that we miss the reason we serve in the first place. We are most effective for God when we find our rest in him. Our physical energy can take us only so far, but the life that Jesus offers will supply us with all we need to complete the adventure he calls us on.

Another lie I believed for many years was that rest was only available on holidays. And yes, holidays are important: they provide time to recharge, time to spend with family and friends, time to explore the world and encounter new people and different cultures. But a peaceful soul is cultivated by daily rest found at the feet of Jesus. The closer we draw to him and the more time we spend with him, the more we will hear his voice and trust him, therefore the more rested we will feel. And then we have the energy, the strength and the courage to take on the world!

Learning to rest at the feet of Jesus is absolutely essential if we wish to live the full and abundant life that God offers us.

Practise pondering

So, we have established how important it is to intentionally build in time to spend with God each day, but this need not always be activity-driven. By this I mean that spending time with God is not always outworked by reading the Bible, praying, worshipping or listening to a podcast. It is also important to take time to simply be quiet before him, to silence those inner voices that are reminding you of all the errands you need to run that day, or the presentation you are rehearsing silently in your head for your big meeting at work tomorrow, and instead to focus on him entirely. We need to learn to reflect and ponder.

Pondering stops us from jumping to immediate conclusions, instead causing us to carefully consider what God says about our circumstances and weigh up our own determinations against the Word of God. Pondering removes our own timeline from what we think God is doing, and focuses rather on who he is and how he is revealing himself to us through our circumstances, our challenges and our conversations with him. Pondering is less about reacting to the "what", and more to do with learning about the *"why"*.

As we practise pondering, the whisper of our Heavenly Father will begin to break through all the white noise of our daily lives. It is in these moments that we enter into a conversation with God and find peace in our circumstances and joy in communion with our Creator.

A. W. Tozer, an American pastor and author who spent his life in the pursuit of God, said: "Coming before God in quietness and waiting upon him in silence can accomplish more than days of feverish activity."[6] Sadly, it took me years to apply this truth in my own life. I was always so busy with feverish activity that I failed to make quiet moments with God a priority. But, in a season when I became so overwhelmed by the busyness of work, ministry and serving in church, I am grateful that God created a window of opportunity for me to sit alone with him for a few hours on a cloudy Sunday afternoon.

There was nothing particularly special about that afternoon. It was cool and cloudy for July. I was visiting a friend for the weekend; we had attended church that morning and were then not sure how to spend the afternoon. We eventually agreed that I would sit on the balcony and journal (feeling the desperate need to reflect on an exhausting two months that had just passed in the blink of an eye), while she had a nap.

I sat there, huddled under a blanket, listening to worship music, and I began to process and reflect upon the busy period that had just passed. It had been stressful, and I felt completely drained, and relieved that it was over. But I did not realize just how desperately I needed this moment of idleness until God graciously gave me the opportunity for it. For three hours I sat alone, staring up at the clouds and watching the light try to break through. I punctuated the time with worship, prayers, reflection, rereading journal entries and writing down new thoughts, as the Holy Spirit inspired me. In just one afternoon, I sat and received God's healing and peace, and allowed his joy to enter into my heart again.

I had had no plan for that afternoon, or a particular agenda or activity that I wished to engage with. I did not come with any specific expectations or seek to focus God's attention on a particular area of my life. Instead, I just sat. I sat and watched planes overhead draw vapour trails across the sky. I emptied my mind and allowed God to direct my thoughts. I didn't say much to him, I simply listened. Moments from the previous weeks flashed across my mind's eye and I began to identify threads of God's grace and guidance through the blur. I didn't ask him any questions, but instead I allowed him freedom to draw my attention to what he considered to be important, not I. And what had previously felt like a season that I had merely survived, having depended on my own strength and abilities and not on God's, was revealed to be full of hidden moments of God's guidance and provision following my afternoon of pondering. What had been hidden to me, as I focused on my feverish activity, was exposed in all its glory when I finally stopped to reflect and ponder the weeks past.

Honestly, I was so drained from all my feverish serving in the preceding months that, in many ways, I had no option but to sit silently, exhausted and worn out, not even knowing what to say to God. And God, in his grace, showed me how valuable moments like that are. This first instance of quiet pondering was a happy accident (if such a thing exists when we trust a Sovereign God), but one that prompted many moments of intentional surrender from that time onwards.

That afternoon was the breath of fresh, Spirit-filled air that I had needed to bring my head back up above the water and be reminded that God holds all things in *his* hands, not in mine. The peace and relief I experienced that day reminded me of the importance of sitting quietly in God's presence and it became a pivotal point in my relationship with my Heavenly Father. From that day on, pondering and reflecting was no longer a rare luxury, but an intentional priority. It was in this environment, seeking God's perspective above my own, that I found peace and joy.

If we are to live the adventure that God has called us to, we must practise pondering. It is in these moments that we are quiet enough to hear the voice of God, reflect on what he is saying and find confirmation and direction for the next step in our journey.

Be thankful

We have already touched upon the importance of cultivating a thankful heart. We live in a society that celebrates instant gratification, so when our desires are not immediately met, we enter a painful waiting game. Often our instinctive reaction is to focus on what we are still waiting for, but with our eyes fixed on that which is absent, we miss the opportunity to recognize and to thank God for all that he has already blessed us with. This perspective breeds discontentment and bleeds our joy.

Discontentment arises when we fail to appreciate the good gifts that God has given us, instead wasting time complaining to him about what we do not yet have. At the root of this problem is the simple fact that we do not trust God to give us what we need, when we need it. But if God has not given us something yet, it is not because he *can't*, but because he does not deem it *necessary* for us right now. Do you trust him?

When we begin to appreciate his love for us and learn to recognize God's hand in the detail of our lives, we realize that what he chooses to give us and when he chooses to give it are perfect. Remember, he is motivated by *love*, not any other lie the enemy would have you believe, and he promises to give us good things. Now, that is not to say he will give us what we want; *his* definition of "good" and *our* definition of "good" may vastly differ. But he does not withhold the things that we want just to spite us; he uses the delay to protect us, to teach us and to ultimately give us something even better than what we ask for.

In my family we are not the most creative when it comes to giving gifts. More often than not, we will circulate a wish list with some items we might like a couple of weeks before a birthday or Christmas, just to provide a few ideas and pointers to other members of the family. At the end of the day, though, it is up to the giver to decide upon which gift to purchase, and to determine how and when they will give it. The recipient does not demand a specific gift or determine when it should be received: they trust the giver. In the same way, we can pray to God and share our desires, but what he chooses to give to us and when he chooses to give it is ultimately his decision, not ours.

In chapter 2 I explained how journaling is a significant part of developing my relationship with God. One of the reasons for this is because I use it to document all my answered prayers. It provides a practical method for me to record God's goodness in my life and see his faithfulness in hearing and responding to my pleas.

Tracking answered prayers has also become a defence strategy against the enemy's lies, because, in those low moments of discouragement and doubt, while I await what I hope for in answer to my prayers, I can turn back the pages of my journal and be reminded of time after time after time when God came through for me. Being reminded of God's faithfulness in my past causes my faith to rise once again to believe he will be faithful in my future.

So what can you thank God for today? Food in the fridge; clean, running water; a roof over your head; a God who loves you? Pause now and show your gratitude for all that he has blessed you with.

Develop godly relationships

God created us to live in community. At the very beginning of the biblical narrative, God created Adam, the first man, but claimed, "It is not good that the man should be alone; I will make him a helper fit for him" (Genesis 2:18). Right from the start, God intended for us to live with companionship. This does not promise marriage to every one of us, but it does promise friendship; there will be people that God brings into our lives in different seasons to help us, to support us, to challenge us and to smooth out some of our rough edges.

It is in community that we learn to celebrate diversity, to work together for a common purpose, and to give and receive encouragement. By including others in our lives and in our decisions, we gain new perspectives and draw from a wealth of experience.

Community is always a group of people, but not every group of people is a community. True community works together for the common good: it builds up, and does not tear down. Community should be a safe place where we can be ourselves, feel accepted, and help to shape and encourage one another. And for better or for worse, we inevitably become more like those we spend most time with. Because we were created for relationship, not isolation, we all have the desire to be part of community, but the challenge is in choosing the *right* community.

Many of the problems we face stem from a lack of good community. While working for a social outreach project in my home city, I met a number of individuals who admitted that a significant reason for their drug habit was because, when they went looking for community, it was addicts that readily accepted them as they were. Several alcoholics we supported had slid into their addiction because they had found company in the pub, rather than sitting alone at home. Mental health issues can arise when thoughts and feelings that could otherwise be shared within community are left unprocessed and internalized due to a lack of safe, trusted individuals to share them with.[7] And how many of us have engaged in relationships, knowing they were doomed from the start, just to feel loved and accepted by someone?

Presently, with the rise of social media and online communication, the value and quality of community is depleting even further. Younger generations are missing out on the opportunity to develop vital social and emotional skills because their community is largely hidden on the other side of a computer or phone screen.[8]

Therefore, we need to make it a priority to build and protect good communities. Our local churches, our small groups and our homes should be places of safety, acceptance and love.

In community we not only bring our gifts for the benefit of others, but we bring our character, our wisdom and our experiences as well. As Christians, it is vital that we find a local church community to be a part of. But within that community, it is also essential to develop intimate godly relationships. These relationships go beyond the trivial and seek to create an atmosphere of trust, accountability, support and encouragement. The Bible states, "As iron sharpens iron, so one man sharpens [and influences] another [through discussion]" (Proverbs 27:17, AMP). True friends do not simply tell us what we want to hear in order to keep the peace, but they provide honest feedback, even if it's hard to hear, because they love us and want the best for us. The process of sharpening can sometimes be painful, but just think how much more effective we can be in our calling if we refuse to fight with a blunt blade.

One of the greatest influences in my own life has been a group of three unassuming girls. They do not have large ministries or special leadership positions; they do not have thousands of social media followers or a plethora of published books (not that there is anything wrong with any of these things); they are simply faithful, humble, prayerful women who willingly serve in whatever their hands find to do.

In 2011, one of these women suggested that three of us meet monthly to pray together. Around a year later, we invited the fourth to join us, and we have met regularly ever since. We use group messages to share prayer requests and answers to prayer. We also enjoy meals together or the occasional spa day. When it is not possible to meet in person, we arrange a group video call so that our connection can be maintained. Simply put, we do life together. We all have different experiences, different testimonies, different perspectives to share and, in so doing, we sharpen one another in our faith.

Since beginning our Prayer Square (as we affectionately call it) we have celebrated incredible miracles together, mourned the loss of loved ones, built one another up in times of difficulty and discouragement. We have witnessed love stories unfold, families grow and God strategically place us where we need to be. Our friendship has spanned oceans as well as years. And I believe I would not be the person I am today without them.

Often we face challenges and are eager for God to answer our prayers, quickly and directly. When we do not have the skills or wisdom to find a solution ourselves, we turn to God for the answer. It is absolutely right that God be our first port-of-call, but sometimes God has already provided for our needs, we just need our eyes opened to see the provision.

There are many examples in the Bible when God's provision is supplied in the friends and family of those called by him. Moses was given Aaron to speak on his behalf, because he struggled with a speech impediment. Ruth served and encouraged her mother-in-law, Naomi, when she was grieving and downcast following the loss of her entire family. King David had his best friend Jonathan to encourage him and give him wisdom when David's future looked bleak. Even Jesus had his disciples to assist him in the practical work he was involved with.

In a nutshell, community is one of God's greatest gifts to us, so we must not neglect it or abuse it. Intentionally building good godly relationships is one of the greatest tools we can carry; not only do we benefit personally, but also, as we work and sow into them, the entire community around us can be encouraged and strengthened in their faith too.

Exercise your faith

Sport and exercise are not really my thing (it seems God forgot to add "motor coordination" the day he made me), but I once entered into a running challenge with a friend. Neither of us had ever run before (aside from school races, a decade or two earlier), so we agreed to run five kilometres three times per week for twelve weeks. We were raising money for Mission Aviation Fellowship and hoping to get fit at the same time.

It was hard work at first, but we made the effort to run together at least once per week, and we soon identified our favourite routes around the city. That first week I had to stop every couple of minutes to catch my breath (yes, I was terribly unfit), but by week two the period I spent running gradually increased as I developed my running technique, improved my breathing and gained stamina.

As time went on, the running became more enjoyable and I celebrated every small improvement. I remember by week ten I was able to run for twenty-five minutes without slowing to a walk—an incredible improvement! And by week twelve, my running had vastly improved and I had lost over a stone in weight. Perseverance, celebrating small victories and support from my friend had got me there.

Our faith can be just like that, too. The more we exercise our faith, the stronger and more resilient it becomes. Every time you face a challenge, choose to engage just a little more faith and a little less fear. As time goes on, your faith "muscle" will strengthen and you will have the ability to face bigger challenges and trust God for greater miracles.

Beth Moore wrote: "We believe little because we see little, so we see little and continue to believe little."⁹ But if we can muster up just a little faith and begin to exercise it, our faith will grow as we start seeing unexpected answers to bigger prayers.

Just as in running, we need to develop perseverance in our faith too. It takes time to build faith and the exercising of it can be a struggle. When fear threatens to overcome you, hold on just a little longer. Just because we are working with God on something does not mean he will do all the work. He does the heavy-lifting, yes, but it takes courage and strength to depend on him when it looks—to us or to others around us—like all hope is lost.

In work and in life, it is important for me to measure progress to keep me motivated, so celebrating the small victories is a vital exercise in keeping me hopeful and focused. Checklists, reflecting and journaling all help to do this. And we can do the same in our faith journey too. Look for the small victories: a change of attitude, a worry that has become less prominent in your mind, or switching your response to challenges from panic to prayer.

My friend and I would regularly send one another selfies from the gym or a photo of our pink, sweaty face after a run, to spur one another on. We both succeeded in the challenge because we supported one another and provided mutual encouragement. It was a little easier to motivate ourselves to fit in another run that week when we knew the other was counting on us to show up. Similarly, our fellow Christians should be the most appreciative and supportive when we are exercising our faith. Our priority is to build one another up, not to get caught up in comparison or envy. When you are struggling to keep the faith in difficult circumstances, reach out to a trusted friend or leader who can encourage you, pray with you, and send you those sweaty selfies to remind you that they are running right alongside you.

If we want to dream big dreams and live the life God intended for us, we have to begin exercising our faith, for without faith it is impossible to please God (Hebrews 11:6). Without faith, we only depend on ourselves. Without faith, we are limited by our own means. Without faith, we cannot enter into a tailor-made, once-in-a-lifetime adventure with him.

If I had laced up my running shoes for the first time and entered straight into a marathon, I would have barely completed the first kilometre. Similarly, if we expect God to ask much of us and use us to do great things for his kingdom, we have to start small. God, in his grace, would not place us straight into a marathon of faith, for, if he did, we would surely fail. We must train for it first.

So start by exercising your faith in small ways. If you do not spot an opportunity right away, ask God to reveal one to you. Ask him to help you, to strengthen you, to give you courage, and believe that he will be with you every step of the way. The more we see him at work in our lives, the more our faith develops.

In his Gospel account, Mark shares what happened when a father brought his son to Jesus for healing. He had already asked the disciples to heal him, but they had been unable to. The father then turns to Jesus and asks that, if he can do anything, to please show his son compassion and help him. Jesus' response, however, was one of frustration. "'*If* you can'! All things are possible for one who believes." Immediately the father of the child cried out and said, "I believe; help my unbelief!" (Mark 9:23–4).

Help my unbelief. How many times have these words crossed your lips? This father was desperate for Jesus to work a miracle in his son, but he first needed the faith that it could be done.

When we bring our requests, our fears, our problems before God, we need to remember who it is we are praying to. He is the God who created the universe, who fashioned everything from nothing. He is the One who masterminded the redemption of mankind through his Son, Jesus Christ. *He can.* Whatever your request is, *he can.* Now, whether or not he will answer in the way we expect him to is another issue, but we will look at that in a later chapter.

Why not begin today by asking God to help your unbelief. Whatever issue is bothering you right now, give it to God in prayer and ask him to do what only he can do. Prise your fingers off and release it to him fully; he can deal with it far better than you can. Take one day at a time and watch God begin to work miracle after miracle in your life as you release it to him and have *faith* that he will act.

Be courageous

To exercise faith, we also need courage. It is impossible for us to live out our God-led adventure without courage.

Being courageous does not mean that fear is absent; there would be no need for courage if we did not face fear. Courage is needed in order to *overcome* fear. We exercise courage when we choose to trust God *more* than our fears. When faced with circumstances that scare us, we can take a deep breath, invite God to bring peace into our hearts and step forward anyway.

"Fear not" is one of the most frequent commands in the Bible. I believe this is because God knows what a terrible thing fear is and how easily we succumb to its tyranny. But God's voice speaks louder: "Fear not, for I am with you; be not dismayed, for I am your God; I will strengthen you, I will help you, I will uphold you with my righteous right hand" (Isaiah 41:10).

In new seasons, we might find the tasks to which God calls us overwhelming. But God is a gracious God, and when he calls us to something, he gives us the grace, the faith, the resources and the ability to respond.

If we are not courageous, we remain in our default: our comfort zone. But in God's kingdom, the comfort zone is a dry, barren spiritual wasteland. Very little grows, very little fruit is produced, and there can be no harvest. If we want to reap a heavenly harvest, it is essential that we muster up courage and begin to take risks in faith.

Learn obedience

As Jesus began his ministry, he travelled from place to place teaching the Word of God. On one such occasion, the people crowded him by the Sea of Galilee, so he borrowed a fishing boat and used it as a platform from which he could continue to teach those that had gathered there to hear him.

When he had finished speaking, he asked the skipper of the boat, Simon Peter, to let down his nets to catch their lunch. But Simon answered, "Master, we toiled all night and took nothing! But at your word I will let down the nets" (Luke 5:5).

Simon Peter was an experienced fisherman and had been working hard all night to find a catch, but to no avail. However, he listened to Jesus and obeyed. On doing so, they caught such a tremendous number of fish that the nets began to break, and they had to call upon their friends in another boat to assist them.

Peter had likely been fishing for most of his life; it's possible that he had learnt the trade from his father before him. In this narrative, he had spent the entire night fishing, depending on his own extensive knowledge, experience and efforts, just trying to earn a living, yet he had nothing to show for it. But at Jesus' word, Peter obeyed, and he immediately received an abundance.

Peter learnt that day that obedience to God is worth far more than our own efforts. When we obey God, no matter how foolish or unlikely the outcome may seem, we will *always* receive an abundance. Obedience to God's Word takes us far beyond where our efforts ever could.

That day, Peter left everything to follow Jesus. Christ famously told Peter that he would no longer be a fisherman, but a fisher of men. Peter, who likely had no schooling, and very little prior knowledge of God, had been called out by Jesus to enter into the greatest adventure, beyond anything he could ever have anticipated.

Peter's obedience to Jesus' request to cast the nets one more time laid the foundation for the far more difficult acts of obedience that Jesus would require of him in the months and years to follow. Yet, upon Peter, Christ promised to build his Church (Matthew 16:18). Similarly, when we respond in obedience to the small acts that God asks of us today, we pave the way for him to ask greater things of us tomorrow. If we are willing to be faithful in the small things, he is willing to trust us with much more (Matthew 25:14–30).

I'm sure Simon Peter had no idea what it meant to be a "fisher of men", but he did not allow that to hold him back from leaving everything familiar and following Jesus. God does not require us to be skilled, only *available* to be used by him. When we walk in obedience to all that he asks us to do, we are choosing to partner *with* him and we will find ourselves achieving far more than we ever thought possible.

Billy Graham, the American evangelist who ministered to over 200 million people in his lifetime,[10] once shared how obedience to the voice of God led his wife on a path different to that which she had envisioned for herself:

> As a young Christian, Ruth, my wife, wanted to be a missionary, as were her father and mother. But God had other plans for her life. Changing circumstances revealed God's will to her, and she was happy where God had placed her. So many of us ask God to change the circumstances to suit our desires, instead of us conforming our wills to his. Don't let circumstances distress you. Rather, look for the will of God for your life to be revealed in and through those circumstances.[11]

Ruth Graham is just one example of an individual who laid aside her own desires to respond to the call of God on her life. Her own plans were honourable and good—she desired to be a missionary, after all—but God had a different plan, a better plan, for her.

We may also have "good" plans and desires for our own lives, but they are still limited by our own finite skills and resources. It is only when we surrender to God's purposes that we push the boundaries of what is possible and enter into the great adventure of faith he created us for.

Follow your convictions

As you press into the life that God wants for you, there will come a time when God asks you to do something that will appear utterly foolish to those around you. And not just to those who do not share your faith in God, but to some of your closest friends and family members too. But there is no need for faith if it does not seem foolish.

If faith made sense, meaning it was explainable and achievable by means of our own, then there would be no need to trust God. That is, no need for faith at all. We all have a choice to live in one of two ways: with faith in God, trusting him to operate and act in realms beyond our own understanding, or to settle for a mediocre existence that can only stretch as far as our own, limited abilities. There is no middle ground. We either hold a conviction deep in our soul that God can be trusted to do what he has said he will do, or we consider ourselves—our own thoughts, decisions and efforts—to be more reliable than God.

When Naaman, a commander in the Syrian army, was told by God's prophet to dip in the River Jordan seven times to be healed of his leprosy, he felt foolish. But God responded to Naaman's obedience and he was healed.

When Abraham and Sarah, each aged nearly one hundred years old, were told by God that they would conceive a son, Sarah laughed at such a foolish notion. But their son Isaac was born the following year.

Hannah, childless and barren, dedicated her hypothetical firstborn son to God, before there was a child to give. The priest reprimanded her foolish behaviour, mistaking her bitterness for drunkenness, but God heard her prayer and she gave birth to the prophet Samuel.

Faith depends on conviction. And conviction is deeply personal. It cannot be used to justify your actions, or to explain your thoughts to others; it can only be held tightly within and followed resolutely. Conviction is that stirring deep within your spirit that urges you forward, even when you do not have the slightest idea of where it might lead you. It manifests itself as boldness and determination, despite your own weaknesses and failings. Conviction believes wholeheartedly that God will do what he has said he will do, and depends entirely on God to reveal the next step.

When God asks us to act in faith, it is highly likely that we will be considered foolish. There is a strong chance that those watching will not understand why we are doing what we are doing. But the bottom line is this: do it anyway. Seek wise counsel and weigh it up against what God says in the Bible, but do not allow popular opinion to sway you. If God calls you to act, follow your convictions and obey him, no matter what people may say or think, no matter how foolish an act it may seem. If it aligns with God's Word and your conviction runs deep, trust him to see it through.

Be led by peace

Learning to cultivate a peaceful heart has been a game-changer for me, and it is so important if we want to fully enter into the adventure we were each created for. When peace reigns in our minds and hearts, each day, each experience, each moment is far more enjoyable, and we are able to face each challenge more readily.

Peace is a fruit of the Spirit and evidence of true faith in God. Even in the midst of difficulty and uncertainty, God can and will still our hearts if we trust in *his* strength, instead of our own. As Lysa TerKeurst puts it: "Trusting God's plan is the only secret I know in the gentle art of not freaking out."[12]

As my relationship with God continues to deepen and my experience of his love and care for me grows, the more easily I find and hold on to peace. Reminding myself regularly of God's love for me and his all-powerful, all-knowing, ever-present nature allows me to more readily identify lies, doubts and fears, and then to reject them. The more we press into the pursuit of knowing God, the more aligned we are with his truth, therefore the easier it is to dismiss fear and to experience a greater peace: one that contradicts our circumstances.

Cultivating a peaceful heart is not about our external circumstances changing, but adjusting our internal conditions to focus on God, and not on our own worries or fears. Deliberation, speculation and calculation are not evidence of God's presence, but rather our own attempts to control a situation, "for God is not a God of confusion but of peace" (1 Corinthians 14:33a).

Philippians 4:6–7 is a well-known passage in the Bible. It states: "Do not be anxious about anything, but in everything by prayer and supplication with thanksgiving let your requests be made known to God. And the peace of God, which surpasses all understanding, will guard your hearts and your minds in Christ Jesus." These verses remind us that God's incredible peace can be ours if we just talk to God about our struggles, rather than trying to deal with them our own way. When we give him permission to enter into our circumstances as opposed to us trying to carry the burden alone, he promises to guard our hearts and minds from stress, anxiety, overwhelming burdens and desperation.

Following the peace in our hearts works hand-in-hand with trusting the conviction in our spirit. While conviction drives action, peace comforts and reassures us during times of waiting, when everything swirls in a blur around us and we are wondering when God is going to step in to calm the storm. His peace—a peace that cannot be given or understood by the world—will be the anchor that encourages us to hold our ground and not to flee in fear.

No matter what we face—concerns about a medical diagnosis, a broken relationship, financial issues, uncertainty about our next step—we can place all these things at the feet of Jesus and ask him to intervene. Then, having invited him into our challenges and having trusted him with them, he will gift us his peace as we wait for him to act. He can do what we cannot: he can carry the burden when it is too much for us, and he can settle the strife in our hearts when the visible evidence around us screams at us to panic, for nothing is impossible with God (Luke 1:37).

Later on in the tale of *The Hobbit*, Gandalf the wizard is asked why he chose Bilbo Baggins, of all people, to participate in such an important quest. "I don't know," he muses, "[Others] believe that it is only great power that can hold evil in check, but that is not what I have found. I've found that it is the small things, everyday deeds of ordinary folk, that keeps the darkness at bay. Simple acts of kindness and love."[13]

Just as Gandalf invited Bilbo to participate in his great adventure, God invites us along on his quest to win the world. He does not call us because of our power, or our influence, or our title, or our wealth (though he can use all of these things), but because our small, everyday acts of kindness and love reveal Jesus' love to the world in the unlikeliest places.

If we prepare ourselves and submit ourselves to God's great plan for our lives, he will engineer opportunities every single day that can reverberate across nations and generations for his glory. Don't just entertain the *idea* of adventure: enter into the fullness of a faith-filled adventure with God. This adventure is not available to us without him, so find a peaceful corner, open your Bible and ask the Father to reveal himself to you today afresh. I promise, you will never be the same again.

5

Facing Opposition

In my late teens and early twenties, I was plagued with sickness after sickness. Nothing serious, usually just the flu. But I would catch it often, sometimes up to four times in one year. These bouts would floor me and leave me with no energy, resulting in weeks off sick from work and, most disappointingly, forfeiting the chance to attend and serve in church.

But as the months and years went on, I began to notice a pattern: I would most often become sick around the same time I would accept ministry opportunities to serve in my local church or help pioneer new initiatives.

Upon this realization, I was then plagued by an even greater sickness: fear. You see, now that I had identified a pattern, I began to anticipate when I might get sick as different opportunities arose. And sure enough, that's exactly what happened.

But it all came to a head in January 2011. It was only one week into the new year; I had already been off sick from work for two weeks over the Christmas period. I had then recovered and returned to my staff role in church for just a few days when another feverish spell hit me during the Sunday morning service and I felt the energy drain out of me once more. I was due to jump up onto the stage after the first worship set to enthusiastically welcome everyone to church and to provide a rundown of the events going on in church that week, but I was struggling to even muster the energy to stand.

As I battled my predicament in my mind, God intervened. The Holy Spirit moved, and the trajectory of the service immediately shifted. The pastor called forth people who needed healing, as the worship team continued far beyond their planned set. Shaking, I stood up from my front row seat, grateful that I did not need to walk far. With tears streaming down my face—tears of frustration and exhaustion—I shared with the pastor's wife what had been running through my head only moments earlier, and she began to pray for me. Yes, she prayed for physical healing, but, most significantly, she prayed that the habit of fear would be broken. And her words filtered through my fear like a ray of sunshine. As we stood together praying at the front of the church, God gave me a vision of him protecting me from the enemy and pointing to the clear path ahead.

In a matter of minutes, as the worship team played the final song in their extended set, the energy returned to my body and joy filled my heart once more. I leapt onto the stage to welcome everyone to church, each of them entirely unaware of the miracle that had just manifested within me. The enemy had used my physical symptoms to distract me from the real weapon: fear. But we had identified it, called it out and conquered it in Jesus' name.

Fear is the modern-day epidemic that is stealing our dreams and opportunities. As I observe the world around me—the rise in terror, turbulent politics, shocking media headlines, provocative posts on social media and conversations with my peers—it pains me to see the fear and anxiety that dominates humanity.

The media has many of us thinking that we can no longer visit big cities for fear of terrorist attacks. The lies and failed promises of politicians have us doubting whether we can trust anyone. I believe we are now so immune to fear and anxiety, that we have also become blind to its effects on us; our increased heart rate and restless sleep, night after night, have become acceptable parts of modern-day life.

But these external influences do not have control over how we *respond* to situations that seek to scare us. As a schoolteacher, I endeavour to teach children on a daily basis how to take responsibility for their own reactions and their own choices. It may not be little Susie's fault that Kim pushed her over, but Susie *can* control how she chooses to respond. If she chooses to push Kim back, then she must also accept responsibility for her own actions; she cannot simply blame everything on Kim. Similarly, we cannot always influence the rough and tumble of life that impresses upon us, but we can maintain control of how we respond to it.

Perhaps we burden ourselves with too much responsibility and try to solve the whole world's problems—effectively trying to adopt the role of God—when we simply need to release these concerns back into his hands. God already has a plan—he has not given up his authority even in the midst of such atrocity—we just need to be quiet enough to listen for his instruction. Fear declares that we do not trust that God is in control. It tells the world that we count our own efforts to be more effective than his.

Overcoming fear is less about us working harder or smarter to solve problems, and more about fighting in the strength that is only available at the feet of Jesus. Imagine how different our world would be if we swapped the amount of time that we spend worrying for time spent in prayer instead?

No matter how big or small the concern is that we bear, we must stop immediately when anxiety begins to swell up within us and talk it through with God. Just talk: it is not necessary to use any fancy language or even to sugar-coat your words. Just tell God exactly how you are feeling. Perhaps, after the first time you share the concern, nothing changes. You still feel tense and anxious. So tell him again. And again. And again . . . until peace begins to dawn in your heart. God hears you, and he *will* respond. God loves his children and never grows sick and tired of hearing their worries and requests. He is infinitely patient with us and it pains him to see us live in a way that is anything but peaceful.

Now, do not misunderstand me; peaceful does not mean uneventful, or even easy. We will all face challenges and difficulties, whether we follow God's best for our life or not. But depending on God, instead of our own understanding, will bring us peace in the *midst* of it. He does not always immediately remove us from the trial, but he promises to be there with us in it. Living at peace is only possible when we trust God entirely, believing him to be the answer to every prayer.

Today's culture champions those who appear to have achieved security, comfort, approval and power. The media would suggest that these things are evidence of a successful and happy life. But if we pursue that which the world values, we will stifle the plans that God has for us. God does not call us to a life of comfort and ease; we are called to fight for the good things that God has prepared for us.

Yet this is not a new problem. The apostle Paul warned the early Christians in Ephesus of the same thing: "Look carefully then how you walk, not as unwise but as wise, making the best use of the time, because the days are evil. Therefore do not be foolish, but understand what the will of the Lord is" (Ephesians 5:15–17).

You see, while God calls us forward into a life of adventure, we sometimes forget that the enemy is determined to throw us off course. While we are content "taking it easy", the enemy has no reason to bother us because we pose no danger to him or his evil plans; this is one of the greatest threats to our Christian journey in the Western world.

We have to *fight* to know God: fight against busyness, against distractions, against the doubt and accusations of others. We have to fight against the lies from the enemy that tell us we are not good enough, not smart enough, not beautiful enough. We have to fight to remain in our adventure.

Fulfilled dreams do not just land on your lap one day. They are the result of relentless effort, overcoming challenge after challenge; they require passion that energizes you to recover from disappointments over and over again, and, inevitably, time. Lots and lots of *time*. But if there is anything that we can be sure of, then it is this: the time will pass anyway. Use it well. Invest every day in the dreams and purposes that God has placed in your heart.

A life with God in no way guarantees a problem-free life. In fact, it is quite the opposite. The Bible assures us that, when we choose to embrace an adventure with Jesus, we will certainly face opposition from the enemy. When we face opposition, we can be encouraged that we are, in fact, doing something right, because the enemy does not bother anyone who is messing up in life all by themselves. Instead, he focuses his attention on those who are choosing to pursue and honour God.

Romans 5:3–5 encourages us to "rejoice in our sufferings, knowing that suffering produces endurance, and endurance produces character, and character produces hope, and hope does not put us to shame, because God's love has been poured into our hearts through the Holy Spirit who has been given to us." Nothing touches us without God's permission, even though it does not always originate from him. But he has given us the tools to fight it, and through it we are built into stronger warriors to fight the good fight of faith.

The biblical account of Nehemiah is a great illustration of the spiritual battle we face daily when we walk in God's purposes. Nehemiah was serving as cupbearer to King Artaxerxes in Susa when he received the report informing him that Jerusalem, the city of his Jewish heritage, was in ruins. Jerusalem, and indeed the whole land of Judah, was in a sad state of affairs following the Babylonian exile initiated by King Nebuchadnezzar around 600 BC.

When Nehemiah heard the news, he was so distraught that he wept, mourned and fasted for days. He prayed for the Jewish people, and he asked God to grant him success when he faced the king, for he wished to return to his home to rebuild the city walls.

God had placed a dream in Nehemiah's heart (Nehemiah 2:12) to rebuild the city and see Jerusalem restored, but from the very start he faced opposition: "But when Sanballat the Horonite and Tobiah, the Ammonite servant, heard this, it displeased them greatly that someone had come to seek the welfare of the people of Israel . . . they jeered at us and despised us and said, 'What is this thing that you are doing? Are you rebelling against the king?'" (Nehemiah 2:10, 19).

These men, feeling threatened by Nehemiah, a man who came bearing letters from the king in opposition to their own desires, were interested only in their own promotion and importance. They employed petty retorts in an effort to discourage Nehemiah, hoping that he would feel foolish or fearful and abandon the vision that God had placed in his heart.

Instead, Nehemiah answered them, "The God of heaven will make us prosper, and we his servants will arise and build, but you have no portion or right or claim in Jerusalem" (Nehemiah 2:20). Come on! Doesn't Nehemiah's response give you goose bumps? I feel my own faith rise every time I read it—words full of power, faith and strength.

Nehemiah did not allow the fear or jealousy of others to dissuade him from obeying what God had asked him to do. God had not only given Nehemiah a practical task to be fulfilled, but he had also placed a burden for his people on Nehemiah's heart and the desire to make his dream a reality. However, Nehemiah needed to engage bravery and courage to see it through.

Representatives from various lands, numerous families and across a spectrum of religious and social standing joined together to build the wall. Amongst them, a wide range of skills and experience was well utilized in restoring the city to its former glory. Individuals from within

Jerusalem itself assisted by working on the wall right on their doorstep. It would seem that everyone could do *something* to help.

But those pesky men, Sanballat and Tobiah, continued to taunt the Jews: What do you think you are doing? Do you really expect to be able to rebuild the wall yourselves? What can you do with a city that lies in rubble? If a fox climbed on this wall it would surely crumble! Your workmanship is terrible!

Yet Nehemiah prayed and continued to dedicate the work to the Lord.

Still unsatisfied that their jeers had failed to scare the Jews, Sanballat, Tobiah and their men grew angry and began plotting a raid to fight the Jews, to disrupt the building work and inevitably leave it in disrepair. Breaching the walls would leave the city vulnerable and weak, exactly what the enemies of the Jews wanted.

Nehemiah had to prepare a defence:

> So in the lowest parts of the space behind the wall, in open places, I stationed the people by their clans, with their swords, their spears, and their bows. And I looked and arose and said to the nobles and to the officials and to the rest of the people, "Do not be afraid of them. Remember the Lord, who is great and awesome, and fight for your brothers, your sons, your daughters, your wives, and your homes." When our enemies heard that it was known to us and that God had frustrated their plan, we all returned to the wall, each to his work. From that day on, half of my servants worked on construction, and half held the spears, shields, bows, and coats of mail. And the leaders stood behind the whole house of Judah, who were building on the wall. Those who carried burdens were loaded in such a way that each laboured on the work with one hand and held his weapon with the other. And each of the builders had his sword strapped at his side while he built. The man who sounded the trumpet was beside me. And I said to the nobles and to the officials and to the rest of the people, "The work is great and widely spread, and we are separated on the wall, far from one another. In the place where you hear the sound of the trumpet, rally to us there. Our God will fight for us."
>
> *Nehemiah 4:13–20*

Notice that Nehemiah did not allow fear of their enemies to stop him from walking in obedience to God's plans. Nor did he choose to ignore the enemy, merely hoping that they would pose no further threat. Instead, he equipped his men with weapons, he was strategic in placing his men at weaker points in the wall and, above all, he encouraged them all in the Lord, reminding them that *God* would be the one to fight for them.

Throughout the day and night, Nehemiah and his men kept watch. They were always armed, always alert, yet continued to work also. They did not choose one or the other—defence or labour—they did *both*.

Nehemiah's enemies continued to attack him, not in a physical and obvious way, but targeting his character, his fortitude and his faith. Time after time, Nehemiah depended on the discernment that God had given him to identify and reject the lies of his enemies. They tried to deceive him and wreck his reputation, but Nehemiah stood firm on his faith in God.

We may not experience attacks in obvious ways either, but that is what makes the offence of the enemy much harder to spot. His offence is chaos, confusion, doubt, busyness, or anything else that breeds anxiety. Like Nehemiah, we too must always be alert for the enemy's schemes which seek to injure our character and decimate our faith, to inject us with fear and derail our unique adventure and purpose.

Remember, John 10:10 states that the enemy comes only to steal and kill and destroy. He is intent on stealing our peace, killing our dreams and destroying our character. His lies speak against all that God says of you: you are loved, you are of worth, you are of value, you hold great potential. Don't let the enemy steal that which God has instilled in you. Claim it back!

But as Nehemiah was so keenly aware, we do not fight this war alone. Jesus Christ defeated the enemy when he died on that wooden cross over 2,000 years ago, then conquered death by rising again three days later. When we surrender our lives to God, as we explored earlier in the book, we are chosen to fight for the winning side. The victory is already ours, but there are still battles to be fought. Are you content with receiving your spot on the winning side, or do you want to minimize the number of casualties at the same time? When we have Christ, we have the victory, but our call is to recruit as many people as possible to live in victory also.

So how do we arm ourselves against the attack of the enemy?

We put on the armour of God

We have already explored in the previous chapter how we can prepare for the great adventure God wants to take us on, but the Bible is very clear that if we truly want to live the full and abundant life that God calls us to, we must dress for battle.

Ephesians 6:10–18 takes us through, step by step, our recommended daily dress code so that we may be able to stand firm against the schemes of the enemy. For, as verse 11 reminds us, we do not fight against flesh and blood, but against evil spiritual forces. The battles we face may manifest themselves in the physical, but our best line of defence is on our knees, calling to the One who, alone, has the power to defeat our enemy.

Our armour is truth, righteousness, peace, faith, salvation and the Word of God. Fists and guns are no use here; we need to reach for something far more powerful. When we value these things and engage them in our daily lives, we can stand strong against the enemy's lies and deceit. When we remind ourselves who the true enemy is instead of pointing blame at others around us, we disarm the evil one and strengthen our relationships instead of allowing them to fall apart. When we raise our shield of faith, we protect ourselves from the fear that the enemy endeavours to instil in us, reminding him of our Victor, in whom our trust lies.

The Bible describes each virtue as being attributed to a different item of armour. This is no coincidence, for we must protect our heart from discouragement, our feet from the long and difficult journey ahead, our minds from lies. But we cannot fight if we only defend. As Nehemiah demonstrated, it is no use just setting up a defence if you forfeit all progress. We must also arm ourselves for the offence with the sword of the Spirit, which is the unerring Word of God.

When we read our Bible, know our Bible, learn our Bible, recite our Bible and allow the Word of God to penetrate our hearts, we ready ourselves for the spiritual fights that we will inevitably face on our adventure.

We learn to discern between the lies of the enemy and the truth of God's voice

This is a big one. So many of us battle with insecurities, comparison, rejection, a feeling of worthlessness; our minds circle over these thoughts time and time again and the enemy wins. He wins by feeding these thoughts and whispering lies that we do not even realize are from him. He wins because we accept these thoughts as truth and disqualify ourselves from any type of adventure for fear of not having what it takes.

But the voice we should be listening to is God's, and this is why delving into the Word of God is so important. The Word of God speaks the absolute truth, and any thoughts contrary to that are lies to be rejected immediately.

However, the truth of God's Word is received in a war zone. The enemy wants us to misunderstand it, to doubt it, to reject it. It is not unusual for godly insights to be met with difficulties. We are at war, and any advance will be met with gunfire. But the artillery cannot destroy us if we are dressed in the armour of God.

Combating the enemy's attack is less about learning to reject his lies, and more about learning to receive God's truth. The more we feed our faith, the less our doubts have to feast upon.

I used to believe a whole host of lies that prevented me from fully embracing the dreams God had laid on my heart. I thought that I was too young and inexperienced, that I lacked the right friends or influence and that I was not holy enough. I believed that I would be no use to God until I was married, or had a family. I compared myself to others and found myself lacking. But God said otherwise.

The voice we must learn to recognize above all others is our Heavenly Father's. When we have a willing heart, he can and will use us right where we are. When we lay our lives in his hands, he can mould us and shape us, promote us and position us, equip us and empower us for exactly what he has called us to do.

Cling to those dreams he has placed in your heart and do not let the enemy steal away your hope. The Bible promises: "So shall my word be that goes out from my mouth; it shall not return to me empty, but it shall accomplish that which I purpose, and shall succeed in the thing for which

I sent it" (Isaiah 55:11). God speaks to accomplish, so if God has said it, it will be. No word of God can fail to achieve its purpose. Hold on to that.

We reject fear and fight with bravery and courage

There is no need for bravery if we do not have any fear to overcome. Bravery plays its part when we act *despite* our fear. Courage is personified when we remember that the outcome does not depend on us, but on God.

Of course we are frightened when we recognize our weakness and feeble attempts at warfare. But no spiritual battle can be fought in the flesh; we must partner with the Holy Spirit himself.

Freedom from the grip of fear is available when we truly place our trust in God. If we understand who God is and how much he loves us, we have no need to fear, for God will be everything we need. We can trust him to act, we can trust him to guide us and protect us, and we can trust him to give us good gifts. We only experience fear when we doubt the character of God. We are afraid when we doubt that God's ways are anything but perfect. But God is right by our side in *everything*, so we must stand firm on this truth and step forward with courage and faith.

Be alert and do not allow fear to steal away the opportunities that God presents you with. When we allow fear to have the louder voice, we miss out on the one-of-a-kind adventure that God has planned for us. Don't you want to live a life full of thrills, suspense and excitement? Wouldn't you like to witness miracles and inexplicable provision on a daily basis? Then we must surrender the fear that we carry.

New opportunities often require bravery, but open doors do not remain ajar for long. If we allow fear and doubt to speak louder than our faith, then we may miss out on what God has prepared for us. God requires us to be strong and courageous.

While working for my local church in Scotland, my role changed quite considerably after about two years of employment there. The change permitted me to continue growing personally, to develop myself and my skillset, to gain new experiences and to expand the teams of staff and leaders within the church. But when I paused to consider the magnitude of that new role, I panicked. Fear gripped me, because I was afraid that I did not have what it would take. I feared the tougher conversations I would have to have, the greater responsibility I would carry and the wisdom I needed to move forward in that role.

The promotion was a privilege, and one that the church leaders had considered me ready for. In the months that followed, they patiently helped me break down the new role into bite-size chunks so that it would not seem so overwhelming, and they sought to encourage me by sharing the potential that they saw in me. However, at the end of the day, I still doubted myself and allowed fear to reign.

I look back on that time now and I am a little sad that I did not embrace that opportunity more readily. I spent a lot of time fighting the change and feeling unworthy, but I had been depending entirely on my *own* ability. If I had only leaned more on God, the challenges I faced would have been far more enjoyable and far more rewarding. If I had only invited God to work through me, I could have achieved far more than the pitiful effort I managed in my own strength. It took me a long time to learn that it is OK—rather, optimal—to simply take one day at a time and fully rely on God.

Spiritual attacks creep up from behind and pounce in our weak and vulnerable moments, so it is important that we have defence strategies already in place. We need quick, go-to ways of dealing with challenges and struggles when they arise so that, when the enemy does attack, we know exactly what needs to be done. It is far more challenging trying to strategize only once emotions are involved.

It proves difficult to think clearly when we are angry or upset or tired and we have not already put effective strategies in place. That is when we make mistakes: we sin, and we try to do things in our own strength. Responding to an attack while plagued by emotions often causes us to make situations worse, not better; they end badly, and other people (or ourselves) get hurt or become bitter. Once resentful, we build an emotional wall—a divide between us and God—and our blame turns upon him. Be careful, because this is exactly what the enemy wants. He is really not that interested in the methods he uses, as long as it achieves the same outcome: distance between you and God.

So we need strategies in place—of knowing how to commune with God on good days—so that when the bad days come, it is far easier to enter into combat. Whether it's an angry retort or an enticing temptation, an absent apology or a fear-fuelled misperception, the tangle of emotions we often experience in these moments can threaten to overcome us. Instead, stop. Take a deep breath. Declare truth. Recite God's Word. Invite God to step in. Worship him and allow the voice of victory to shout louder than the voice of pain or defeat. Remind yourself of what God has already spoken over you and allow words of truth to penetrate your heart.

Soon, you'll begin to notice your heartbeat slowing, your tense muscles relaxing and your tears drying up. The peace of God, that surpasses all understanding, will engulf you, and your perspective will correct itself as your focus shifts from your friend, your family member, your colleague, or whoever you might be thinking of as the perpetrator and you recognize the true enemy at work in your heart, seeking to destabilize you and discourage you.

Resist allowing the well of emotions within you to rise or to take root in your heart, growing weeds of bitterness and resentment. Resist succumbing to temptation to temporarily satisfy a need. Resist responding to someone with sharp retorts, intent on hurting them like you have been hurt. If we have no defence strategies in place, we could respond impulsively and make the situation worse.

Therefore, take time to equip yourself with go-to defence strategies: memorize Scripture, keep a few songs of praise on your phone or in your car, and learn to recognize the voice of the enemy, so that you are prepared to weed out the lies from amongst truth. We do not have the power or strength to combat him ourselves, but we do have direct access to the One who does. God in us is the only way to fight.

Nehemiah also had his defence strategies in place, and he knew that God was with him. When they had finished building the wall just a couple of short months later, fear entered the hearts of Judah's enemies because they recognized that the wall had been completed, not by the hands of men, but by the hand of God.

Though the wall was now built, there was still much for Nehemiah to do, and he continued to walk in obedience to all that God asked him to do. He placed guards at every gate to the city, always remaining alert for the enemy, and he began to rebuild the city itself. He accounted for all the people of Israel, each according to his own tribe, and ensured they each had a place to live. He, with the prophet Ezra, educated the people in the Word of God and called them to repentance and worship.

God had called Nehemiah, not only to rebuild the physical, but the spiritual too. Through Nehemiah's obedience to God, Israel was re-established as a great nation once again. Yes, he faced attacks. Yes, he faced opposition. But he knew his God and chose faith over fear. And his obedience and trust were greatly rewarded.

Throughout history, God's soldiers have faced (and will continue to face) opposition and hardship, but God's Word warns our oppressors: "Keep away from these men and let them alone, for if this plan or this undertaking is of man, it will fail; but if it is of God, you will not be able to overthrow them. You might even be found opposing God!" (Acts 5:38–9).

And when God acts, he rarely does so in a way that we expect or that makes sense. God saves in his own way, not necessarily in the ways that we can identify with. Facing opposition requires strength, courage and determination. We need to stand firm on God's promises and look fear full in the face. The only way to overcome fear is to acknowledge it, name it, call it out and tackle it with the strength available to us through the Holy Spirit. It is less important that we know *how* our challenges will be overcome, but essential that we understand *who* will overcome them.

No matter what attack we face, we *can* overcome when we arm ourselves against the enemy's schemes. When we belong to God, we can rest because he has already won the victory. God will fight for us, if we only let him. Psalm 34:19 reminds us that "many are the afflictions of the righteous, but the Lord delivers him out of them all". So do not get so blinded by the physical circumstances that you fail to recognize the spiritual forces at work. We must spiritually equip ourselves so we can claim the spiritual victories. There is no other way to truly overcome hardship. There is no other way to claim ground. There is no other way to advance forward.

6

Embracing Challenge and Change

The morning of 28 December 2011 felt like any other. I was enjoying a few days off work between Christmas and New Year and had savoured a longer lie in bed that morning. However, on rising, I was shocked to discover an unusual lump in my left breast. Understandably, it shook me a little, but I was determined not to worry about it until I had had it checked out. I immediately called the doctor's surgery and was disappointed to learn I would have to wait eight weeks for an appointment.

As a flurry of thoughts entered my mind, I picked up my Bible. The Scripture for that day determined by my reading plan was Deuteronomy 30:11–20, entitled "Choose Life". As I read, I was particularly encouraged by verse 19, and claimed it as a promise over my life: "I call heaven and earth to witness against you today, that I have set before you life and death, blessing and curse. Therefore *choose life*, that you and your offspring may live" (emphasis added). In that moment, faced with uncertainty and worry, I prayed to God and claimed life in my circumstances. I refused to let the thought of what could be steal my peace.

At the end of February, I attended the appointment at my doctor's surgery and was referred to the breast clinic at the hospital for further tests. A week or two later, while I still awaited an appointment at the clinic, still carrying in my mind questions and concern, I sat in the weekly prayer meeting at church. The focus that evening was on healing, and I slowly raised my hand to receive prayer. For the weeks since I had first felt the lump, I had regularly and intentionally declared Deuteronomy 30:19 over myself and repeatedly claimed life. And as I sat in the basement room in church with a small group of people huddled around me, praying for healing in my body, I claimed life once again.

As they prayed, I began to feel an unusual sensation around the lump; it was tingly, and felt like hot, molten lava was bubbling away under my skin, as if the lump was melting away. I was desperate to feel it to check, but thought it best to wait until I was somewhere a little more private to do so! As soon as the prayer meeting was over, I darted to the bathroom and found that the lump felt considerably smaller.

A couple of weeks later, I experienced the same sensation during a church service, and by the time I attended my clinic appointment the lump had gone. The doctors performed a series of tests and scans and found nothing.

When unexpected circumstances interrupt our lives, we rarely have control over the issues we face, but we do have control over how we choose to respond to them. When I felt that lump, I could have instantly jumped to conclusions of what could be; I could have spent those weeks full of worry and anxiety, imagining the worst. But how would that have helped? Instead, I didn't allow my circumstances to defeat me; I ran to the God who heals, who provides, who comforts and who strengthens.

Everyone faces hard seasons in life but our attitude dictates what happens next. The way we choose to *respond* to those challenges determines whether we live in peace or in fear.

How often do you get frustrated because things don't go the way you planned? Or inconveniences discourage you and cause you to question whether or not God really does have everything under control? How do you feel when a situation appears to get worse, not better?

It may be possible to keep up a demeanour of confidence and trust when everything in life is dandy, but in the face of challenge or disappointment, what we truly believe about God will come bursting out, exposing our raw faith. The unmasking will be painful, and most likely reveal weakness and vulnerability, but by uncovering the very bedrock of our beliefs God finds a foundation upon which he can begin to build. This is essential work, for the size of our dreams, of our purpose, of our destiny is determined by our understanding of the size of our God.

Mountain-top experiences are great, aren't they? For this is often where God reveals himself to us and encourages us, or speaks promises over us. I'm sure we all love a mountain-top experience. But there is just one problem: nothing grows on the mountain-top.

Following a mountain-top experience, God most often leads us down into the valley to be readied for whatever he revealed to us on the mountain. It is only in the valley, after all, that things grow. It is here that our character is shaped and our faith is stretched, and God uses the harder things in life to prepare us for what is still ahead. In these times of difficulty, we are reminded of our desperate need for God and it encourages us to run back into his arms.

It can be so easy to let indifference creep back into our walk with God while we live in (and enjoy) a season on the mountain-top. But God has something to say to us in every season and we must choose to consistently surrender to him, no matter what we are facing.

Time and time again I have been encouraged by passages in the Bible that reveal God's hand in the detail of our lives, even through difficult seasons and uncertainty. Take Gideon, for example. Gideon was a man who lived his life in fear. We first meet him in Judges 6; the son of Joash was busy beating wheat in the wine press and hiding from the Midianites when God paid him a visit.

"The Lord is with you, O brave man," God said to Gideon (Judges 6:12b, AMP). Brave? *Really?* This was a man who beat wheat in a wine press for fear of what the Midianites would do to him; he obeyed God's commands under the protection of darkness, afraid of what his own family and friends would think; he repeatedly asked for signs of confirmation from God, just to be *sure* of what God had asked him to do. But what I love here is that God spoke life and strength over this man who was yet timid and afraid. You see, when God speaks over us and declares who we are and who he created us to be, we have no reason to be afraid.

Then Gideon begins to ask the questions we have all thought at one time or another:

"If the Lord is with me, why has this happened to me?"

"God, why haven't you come through for me yet?"

"Lord, show me a sign you are really with me."

"Go in this strength of yours . . . " was God's response (Judges 6:14, AMP). Um, what strength? Gideon does not appear to be demonstrating much strength here! God had called Gideon to save his people, the Israelites, from the oppression of Midian, but Gideon faced this challenge with much fear and uncertainty. Yet throughout Judges chapters 6 and 7,

God graciously encourages Gideon and takes him through the plan one step at a time. Gideon may not appear to us to be up to the task, but he was God's chosen man. God had created Gideon and knew him intimately, and, despite his sensitive disposition, Gideon was the right man for the job because God had said he was. Period.

Gideon's fear did not disqualify him for the very purpose he was created for. The Spirit of the Lord was with him (Judges 6:34) and empowered him to do what God had asked him to do. Gideon may have been afraid, but he didn't run or try to hide. He remained at God's side.

Then Gideon asks for confirmation: a sign (well, two signs actually) that would prove that God had really meant what he had said, and Gideon could reassure himself that it was not just some foolish idea in his head. Yet God was gracious again, responding to both of Gideon's requests.

Only then, after God had encouraged Gideon, strengthened him as a leader and built up his faith, did God begin to align him for the purpose he was created for. Gideon's fear became the catalyst that turned him from wimp to winner, from coward to conqueror. God spent time preparing Gideon and waited until he was ready before leading him into his adventure. The same is true of us; the incredible blessing and purpose that God has for us up ahead is too great for us as we are now. We must persevere through the challenges and press ahead, allowing God to prepare us and lead us into all that he wants to give us in the future.

At that time, Gideon had a huge army at his disposal, but God knew that if the entire army entered into the battle, they would claim the victory for themselves and not have the ability to see God's hand in it. Therefore, God began to whittle down the crowd . . .

Using a series of seemingly insignificant details, God began to instruct Gideon to send men home. Those who were afraid were the first to go. A detail as small as how they chose to drink their water was also used to sift out who would stay and who would leave. In a matter of hours, the army was streamlined from 32,000 all the way down to just 300 men.

God reassured Gideon and strengthened him one more time by leading him secretly into the enemy's camp. There, Gideon overheard chatter amongst the Midianites that God had already revealed the impending victory to some of them in a dream. Only then was Gideon ready to do what God had called him to do, what he had been created and purposed for. Now Gideon would lead the Israelites to victory.

At Gideon's word, the 300 men surrounded the enemy camp, blew their horns, smashed pots and shouted victory to the Lord. On hearing the sudden, tremendous noise, the Midianites panicked and God caused them to turn on one another in the confusion, killing many. Some fled, but Gideon and his men pursued them, despite their exhaustion, and eventually subdued the Midianite army, bringing peace to the land once again.

Gideon was no perfect specimen—none of God's chosen instruments ever are—but Gideon's testimony reminds us that God can use us despite our fear and lead us safely through trials and difficult seasons, as long as we are willing to take steps to obey him. God is gracious and patient with us. He will reassure us, strengthen us and help us overcome our fears. The more we obey God and see his provision, the more fearless we will become.

Sometimes God will whittle us down and temporarily weaken us (permitting illness, redundancy, financial crisis, isolation) so that his victory can be all the greater. But we must not panic in these moments, thinking God has abandoned us. His power is made perfect in weakness (2 Corinthians 12:9), and he works all things for *his* glory, not ours.

Gideon surrendered to God's way, though it perhaps seemed ludicrous at the time, and God won him the fight. Despite feeling ill-equipped for the challenge set before him, Gideon faithfully responded in obedience to all that God had called him to and God provided everything that he needed.

When we surrender to God and allow him to work in our lives, despite our fears, doubts and inabilities, he *will* act. Our difficulties pose no challenge to God; we can trust his capability, his willingness and his timing. If God calls us to act, then we should obey and trust God to outwork what he chooses. Our responsibility is only to obey; God is responsible for the outcome of our obedience to him.

Gideon and his army lifted their voices to God and the battle was won. We, too, are victorious when we lift our voices in prayer and praise instead of being overwhelmed by the circumstances around us. God is mighty to save, whatever the situation. When we charge headlong into challenge with faith and determination, we pave the way for a miracle. When nothing is certain, anything is possible.

Growing up, I loved to hear stories of men and women of God in all walks of life and every corner of the earth who had witnessed great miracles. Their stories of adventure and wonder inspired me to live an abandoned life of faith because I wanted to experience God's power for myself. I, also, wanted to have stories to tell of miraculous provision, overwhelming coincidences that were anything but coincidental, and God-ordained, last-minute, in-the-nick-of-time intervention from heaven.

But what we often fail to acknowledge is that, in order to have a great testimony, we must first be greatly tested. We hear these incredible stories only once they have ended happily-ever-after. We find that we want a miracle but resent the circumstances that require one. So how do we deal with tests when we are in the midst of them, not knowing yet how they will end?

Well, we remind ourselves of who God is. God cannot lie (Hebrews 6:18), therefore we can trust what he says about himself in the Bible. He is all-knowing (Isaiah 40:28), all-powerful (Matthew 19:26) and faithful (Hebrews 10:23). He is the Creator (Genesis 1:1), the Provider (Genesis 22:14), the Healer (Exodus 15:26) and the Comforter (2 Corinthians 1:3–5). God is a Loving Father (1 John 3:1), a Mighty Warrior (Zephaniah 3:17) and a Just Judge (Psalm 94).

Psalm 34:17 assures us that, when the righteous cry for help, the Lord hears and delivers them out of all their troubles. In John 14:27, Jesus promises: "Peace I leave with you; my peace I give to you. Not as the world gives do I give to you. Let not your hearts be troubled, neither let them be afraid."

Clinging to these truths has carried me through many difficulties, none more so than when I faced a particularly challenging set of circumstances as I pursued my God-given purpose.

I grew up in Scotland, studied there and worked in a couple of different ministries in my home city, but, at thirty years old, I felt God direct me towards Germany. God provided very few details when he first called me, but it was everything I needed in order to take the first step: I moved to the country to learn the language and the culture.

I found a good language school not too far from the handful of people I already knew in Germany (I thought that would be a good place to start) and applied to join the beginners' course. From there, accommodation was found, a one-way flight was booked and I submitted my resignation at work.

There were many "unknowns" that would be faced in the following months: which church would I attend, who would I build friendships with, how long would it take to learn the language, what comes next once I have learnt the language? However, the one question I was asked the most was, "How will you financially support yourself?"

Honestly? I didn't know. Finding a job without knowing the German language was a near impossible task. But I stood firmly on the promise that God is a God who provides, and if he had called me to Germany (which I firmly believed he had), then he would also have these other details figured out too.

But four and a half months in, having spent all of my money, including the little savings that I had, I woke one morning to discover I had only one penny left in my bank account.

I had always endeavoured to steward my money well, but circumstances out of my control had crippled my finances further. Most significantly, the tenant living in my property in Scotland announced he was moving out, giving just three weeks' notice, despite his contract not due to end for another seven months. This would result in having a mortgage to pay for in Scotland as well as rent on my apartment in Germany. These circumstances were less than ideal, but rather than throwing a strop, I clung to the promises of God's provision.

At first, I thought that surely God would come through for me by the time my Scottish tenant had moved out of the apartment . . . but that day came and went.

Then I knew he would *definitely* have to provide for me before my mortgage payment was deducted a few days later . . . then he missed that deadline too, causing my bank account to plummet into my overdraft.

Hours ticked by that day as I refreshed my mobile banking app more than regularly, just in case I had "missed" the miracle. My increasingly insistent prayers and positive declarations of faith appeared to be bouncing off the ceiling and going no further. The previous week I had assured my church home group that I would have a miracle to report by the following weekend. How would I tell them that I had been sorely mistaken? Very quickly, the strong, resilient faith that I had been holding firmly in place since arriving on the continent began to fall apart.

In the days that followed, I experienced every emotion possible. It began with anticipation and excitement for the expected miracle, which soon turned to doubt, then spiralled into fear and anxiety like I had never experienced before. I became so anxious that I spent several days fighting the physical manifestations of it.

But where was God in the midst of this? I had trusted him, had I not? I had given up everything to follow his call, so why had he not come through yet? Would he really leave me with nothing?

That week felt long, and exhausting. But I learnt three valuable lessons:

God provides one day at a time

Even though it felt that God had abandoned me, or not provided for me as he promises in his Word, I began to realize that I had had what I needed for each day. He had provided enough food for me for *that day*. He had provided grace for me to cope with what I faced *that day*. There was no point dwelling on tomorrow, or next week, for God promised that that provision would come when I needed it. I had been looking for a miracle that would meet my needs for the coming weeks or months, but, as Oswald Chambers said, "You cannot hoard things for a rainy day if you are truly trusting Christ."[14]

God's timing is perfect

In hindsight, I realize that I began to panic, not because I doubted that God would come through, but because I felt that God was *late*. Yet that was according to a timeline that *I* had concocted, not him. Trusting his provision also means trusting his timing—this is never a fun lesson, no matter what we are waiting for! But his timing is wrapped up in grace, protection and glory too. God is never in a hurry, but he is never late.

God uses our weakness to reveal his glory

Just like Gideon's army, God will sometimes strip back the worldly provision we come to depend on so that our focus returns to him. We can become blinded to his goodness when we only see provision in pay cheques, pension schemes or a clean bill of health from medical staff. But when those things fail us, God lovingly draws our attention back onto him, to witness his miraculous provision, so we no longer wrongly accredit it to perishable things.

I was reassured that God is faithful, he loves me, he cares for me, he had heard my prayers, he knew what I needed and he was (and still is) capable of providing for me for he is a good Father. When we trust him, we do not need to do anything to *earn* his love or provision; it brings him joy to give us his *best*.

No sooner had I reflected on my situation and learnt these lessons than God began to act.

The very next day, a Monday (ten days after my Scottish tenant moved out and five days after my mortgage payment had been deducted), I received an email from former missionaries offering me wisdom and guidance, having faced similar challenges themselves. I am so grateful that God's provision is not just financial; finance is only a means to an end, after all. His provision extends to people, resources and opportunities too. These are the things that truly bring wealth.

Later that evening, I was contacted by friends in Germany and informed that an acquaintance of theirs—whom I had never met—had heard of my challenges and wanted to financially support me . . . for an entire year. I cried.

On Tuesday, friends in Scotland called me, requesting my bank account details, for they also wanted to send me money and begin supporting me monthly.

On Wednesday, I attended my church small group and was then able to share with them how God had provided. It was the testimony that I had indeed hoped to have shared with them, but it had looked so unlikely just a few days previously.

On our way home in the car, I shared with my group leader that the mortgage payment that had been deducted from my account the previous week had taken me into the red, since I received no rent from my tenantless apartment that month. He prayed, asking God to expunge the overdraft, as we sat waiting for the traffic lights to turn green.

On Thursday, I received a letter from the bank informing me that I was overdrawn (yes, I had been well aware, thank you) and that fees would be deducted for every day I had been (and would continue to be) overdrawn. That evening, feeling dejected at the thought of further financial loss, I logged on to my online banking platform and found that a further two financial gifts had been transferred into my account without my knowledge, bringing me back into the black, and even covering all the fees I had incurred. I cried again.

That was a hard season (albeit a season that only lasted two weeks but felt like a lifetime), but God proved himself faithful at every challenge I faced. It became the testimony that fuelled my faith in all future financial challenges, knowing God could and would provide for me again, just as he had done before. I learnt that he works for us behind the scenes, lovingly caring for our every need, even when we don't see it or appreciate it ourselves. His love for us is so great, so deep and so personal. His timing is spot on, always. And he never abandons us; we simply need to call out to him, and he meets us right where we are.

Without that turbulent week, I could never have truly appreciated the extent to which God goes to surprise us and reveal to us how much he loves us. I would have missed his hand in the detail of my life. He shows his Word to be true and himself to be faithful. And others then had the opportunity to partner with me and sow into the adventure he had taken me on.

Whatever you are facing right now, be assured that God loves you, he is for you, and he is ready and willing to work a miracle in your life; just call out to him and watch him act. No challenge is too great or too small for him to take an invested interest and lead you safely through it.

But aside from challenge, change can also disrupt our lives and stir up a whirlwind of emotions. Change is inevitable in life, but some of us handle it better than others, especially if it is a change we did not want or expect.

Perhaps, for you, change has manifested as marriage, a new baby, a different career or an illness to be faced. Navigating change takes hard work, expends much energy and raises many questions.

"How will change affect me?"

"How will life be different for my family after this change?"

"What about my . . . home, job, finances, [fill in the blank]?"

Can you relate?

God often brings about change *around* us to bring about change *in* us. He does not do it to stress us out or panic us, but he uses it as an object lesson to draw our eyes back onto himself so he can grow and shape us, preparing our character, our faith and our perspective for all that he has prepared for us in the next season of life.

He places us in situations that are completely out of our control, so that he can remind us and demonstrate to us that *he* is the one in control. We were never really in control to begin with, but we do like to interfere from time to time, don't we?

I have always been very independent. I am a bit of a "Jack of all trades" and can put my hand to just about anything and get an acceptable result. I achieved good grades at school without trying all that hard; I hold some skill in music, art, photography, DIY, computing and web design, among other things; I have experience working with all ages of children, teenagers and adults; and I have always been well organized, trustworthy, reliable and committed. Thanks to this wide range of skills, I was offered many opportunities and, more often than not, thrived in them: in work, in church and in life.

Maybe you immediately see the problem with this, but I did not. Not for a long time, anyway. The problem is that, because of my varied skillset, I always depended on my *own* ability and achieved much. I had never really experienced the need to seek God's help. I had always muddled through on my own . . .

Until I moved to Germany.

It was not just financial need that proved a challenge. All of a sudden, the easiest of tasks were a hundred times harder. Because I had very meagre German language skills to begin with, even my weekly visit to the supermarket rendered me fearful. My heart would pound as I shuffled closer to the cashier, not knowing what they might ask me and having no way to respond anyway. On several occasions I bought the wrong items because I had entirely misunderstood the label.

Meeting new people and building friendships takes time and is hard enough without the added language barrier. My first friendships could only grow as far as the other person's ability in English permitted, because I was unable to communicate or express myself at all in German.

I had to familiarize myself with a new country, a new culture, new laws and legislation, new cities, a new church, new currency, a different transport system. This is when I truly learnt to depend on God. Like it or not, he was all I had. But I soon discovered that he was all I needed.

I soon began to recognize his hand in the small and mundane events of the day. His timing was impeccable, he orchestrated numerous "coincidences", and he lovingly caused my path to cross with the right people just when I needed them the most. I was dependent on him for understanding the language, for financial provision, for opportunities to build friendships and for direction as I navigated my way around unfamiliar territory. For the first time in my adult life, I had nothing in and of myself to depend on; I had to completely rely on God.

I remember the first day I went to church. It was in a different city and required a train and two buses to get there. The previous day I had carefully mapped out the route, noted down the departure times and memorized the bus numbers. So, bright and early the next morning, I began my journey.

Thankfully, the train ride passed without a hitch. As the train slowed into the station, I was poised at the door, ready to disembark the moment the doors opened, knowing that I only had four minutes between the train arriving and the first bus departing.

I trotted up the platform, keen not to waste a second, my eyes frantically scanning the unfamiliar station for the exit. The problem was, there were several exits.

I knew I needed to reach Bus Station A, but no signs in the train station made any reference to buses, let alone Station A. On my second attempt I found the correct exit and was pleased to find that Station A was that which was closest to me. I wasn't pleased, however, that Bus 37, that I had so eagerly sought, had already departed.

I stood there, pleased that I had made it to the correct city, but dejected at the idea that I was so close to church, yet entirely unfamiliar with my new surroundings and no idea how to complete my journey.

At first I thought, "Well, you made it this far, that's a good start. At least this part will be familiar when you try again next week." But another voice in my head reasoned: "But you made it *this far*! Isn't there another way to reach your destination?"

My newly acquired German SIM card had very little data availability on it, and I had already exceeded the limit due to still having no Wi-Fi set up in my apartment. Therefore the search for a new bus route was a slow and frustrating one. After about ten minutes, the webpage successfully loaded and presented me with a new bus route and departure time. It would cause me to be a few minutes late for church, but that was a compromise I was willing to make.

The newly anticipated bus arrived a short time later and, knowing I had to change buses at "Berliner Straße", I kept my eye on the information screen and my thumb hovering over the "stop" button. At the bus stop on Berliner Straße, it was a very easy hop-off-one, hop-on-another switch, and I once again kept my eyes glued to the information screen, determined not to miss my final stop.

Eventually, the screen announced: "Next stop: Habichtweg", and I leapt off the bus with great excitement and anticipation to finally visit the church that I had been streaming online and praying into for several months previously.

But where was the church? Yes, the travel app had taken me to the correct bus stop, but as I rotated 360 degrees on the spot, I realized I had no idea where to go next.

"God, what now? You've taken me this far; show me where to go."

There was a huddle of young-ish, trendy-ish people that had got off the bus with me, and something inside of me told me to follow them. So I did.

As I walked a couple of strides behind them, I wondered how long I could follow them without appearing too conspicuous. There was no-one else around, and we appeared to be walking away from the residential area towards several business premises, so it made sense to me that this group had a valid reason for being there. I kept up my tail.

Just as I was beginning to doubt my plan, we rounded a corner and I spotted parking stewards wearing hi-vis vests, lining the road to the church entrance like lights on a runway. Despite uncertainty, failed plans and no language to ask for help, I had successfully reached my destination, with more than a little help from the Holy Spirit.

Interestingly, it wasn't until another month or so later I realized just how much the Holy Spirit had helped me that morning. One Sunday I successfully caught Bus 37 and discovered that it did stop on Berliner Straße, as expected, but at a junction some distance away from where I needed to catch the next bus. Had I taken Bus 37 that first Sunday, I would have faced even more difficulties trying to identify the street and direction I needed to walk in in order to find the second bus stop and may have never made it to church at all. It is in small details like these that I am now so acutely aware of God's guidance in everyday, mundane activities.

Yet the challenges we face, and the weaknesses and failings we have, are no accident; God uses them all to lead us to himself. When we do not have the skills, character or provision to take the next step, our lack should propel us towards his abundance, and not to anxiety. Fear swells within us when we think everything depends on us, but God uses our weakness to remind us that everything actually depends on him.

One of the primary reasons we find ourselves worried or stressed is because we are thinking about the future: weeks, months or even years ahead. Our scenarios are often theoretical, yet our anxiety is very real. But if we learn, instead, to focus on today—embrace it, enjoy it and engage fully with it instead of thinking too far ahead—our anxiety often disperses. The Bible encourages us to "not worry about tomorrow; for tomorrow will worry about itself. Each day has enough trouble of its own" (Matthew 6:34, AMP).

When we learn to live in the moment, our eyes and our spirit are more alert to the little surprises that God engineers throughout our day. We begin to see his hand at work in the routine tasks, or recognize his guiding hand steering us away from trouble. Those things we once considered to be coincidences we no longer perceive just as luck, but as personalized gifts from heaven to brighten our day.

What is God asking you to do today? Not tomorrow, not next week, but *today*? There is nothing to be achieved in asking God for direction in our futures if we are not obedient in that which he has already asked of us. Until we can be trusted to obey God in the now, he will not trust us with what is coming next.

When we commit our lives to God, we also commit to being obedient to what he asks of us. But sometimes we are slow to understand what this actually means. We are looking for great sea-worthy adventures on the vast ocean of unknowns, but that will never be available to us unless we are first willing to get our feet wet and learn to be obedient in the small, simple acts of every day. If we commit to being obedient to God, then we commit to following through on the smallest or the largest thing; our attitude should be the same to both.

Yes, we should be dreaming big dreams. But dreams are not fulfilled with just a hop, skip and a jump to the finish line. Anything worth building takes much time and many, many small incremental steps towards success. So do not overlook the significance of the small steps of obedience you are taking (or maybe not taking) each day. 1 Corinthians 15:58 reminds us to be steadfast, immovable, always abounding in the work of the Lord, knowing that in the Lord our labour is not in vain. Every seed planted and nurtured will, one day, bear great fruit.

When we love someone, we seek to do what will please them, and act without hesitation. So why should it be any different with God? If we wholeheartedly love our Heavenly Father, then we will want to live in a way that pleases him, and therefore obey him without question.

We can expect God to ask us to do things that appear unattractive or scary, and it will take great courage and faith, sometimes, to take that step of obedience. But once we do, his grace and strength fills us like never before and the tasks he sets before us become divinely easier when we rise to the challenge and obey his commands. Surrendered obedience to God is the only path to true joy.

Stopping to remember God's faithfulness to us in our past builds our faith for what he will do in our present struggles. Sometimes it is difficult to imagine that the same God who performed every miracle in the Bible can and will step in and do the impossible in our lives too. But, if we allow him to, he loves to surprise us and overwhelm us with his provision.

I have a friend who, while studying, returned to his school dormitory one day to find that his laptop was broken. And not just a little broken; it was broken in two. Disgruntled and frustrated at this misfortune, he—in his own words—responded like a child and had a little tantrum. Then, lying down on his bed in resignation, he fell asleep. An hour or so later, he received a knock at his dorm door; it was his classmate. "Come with me," he told my friend. Along the corridor, in his dormitory, the classmate pointed to his own laptop, only a few months old, and said, "For the last three days, God has been prompting me to give this to you."

Our perspective can be so limited, can't it? We see what is right before us and respond—often poorly—to what is evident to our own eyes, but God is at work in places *unseen*. God was working on the provision of a new laptop for my friend before it was even broken! That is how good our God is. He is right there with us in every challenge and change, showing us the way forward, if we only have the eyes to see it. He is loving, caring and forever faithful.

In his second letter to the church at Corinth, the apostle Paul wrote, "But he said to me, 'My grace is sufficient for you, for my power is made perfect in weakness.' Therefore I will boast all the more gladly of my weaknesses, so that the power of Christ may rest upon me. For the sake of Christ, then, I am content with weaknesses, insults, hardships, persecutions, and calamities. For when I am weak, then I am strong" (2 Corinthians 12:9–10).

The apostle Paul is testifying to the early church that he faced many challenges of his own, and walking in obedience to God was no easy option, even for him. But (yes, there is a big "but") he states that he is content because he understands that it is only through his own weaknesses that God's power and glory is most evident. He boasts of his own failings, because he knows that it creates even greater scope for the Holy Spirit to work in him and through him. Paul's attitude was one of joy and perseverance, because he embraced a higher perspective: one which looked beyond his own circumstances.

If we are truly committed to fully participating in the adventure that God has called us to, we too must adjust our attitudes and seek a greater perspective for the good of all, and not just ourselves. Only then can we face change and challenge head-on and embrace the opportunities for preparation and growth that come with them.

7

The Waiting Game

I remember the night well. It was 2006, and I was sitting in church during a youth service, sitting at the back-right of the dimly lit hall. One light shone brightly, illuminating the gentleman speaking at the front. He shared his experiences of many years on the mission field in southern Italy, and my heart was stirred.

Overseas mission and the life of a missionary had always fascinated me. I grew up hearing the incredible true stories of great men and women of faith, such as David Livingstone and Jim and Elisabeth Elliot, who gave everything to spread the love of Jesus to those who had never experienced it.

As a family, we often hosted missionaries who visited the UK, and even my own uncle spent a number of years on the mission field in Brazil.

As soon as I was old enough, I signed up to participate in short-term mission teams: firstly around Scotland, then further afield in countries across Europe. Barely a year went by through my teens and twenties when I failed to spend time as part of a short-term mission team.

So that night, at just nineteen years old, when God whispered into my heart his call on my life to overseas mission, I welcomed his purpose with great anticipation. I would daydream about where God might send me and I very nearly quit university the following summer, ahead of my second year, to go to Bible College instead. But that was not God's intended path. As the years passed, my expectation dwindled, and I began to doubt what God had said or, indeed, wonder if I had already missed my opportunity.

I was working as a physics teacher in a respected high school when, in 2010, I was approached by my pastor and invited to join the staff team at church. With an invitation into full-time ministry, I recall thinking that

I must have *misunderstood* God all those years previously . . . Yes, that must have been it. He had surely called me into full-time ministry, not to overseas mission.

Having then been appointed as Operations Manager, I thought I had made it. I was working in full-time ministry—living my dream!—so I considered it time to settle down, start a family, live locally and serve the church for the rest of my days.

I didn't feel I had compromised in any way; after all, I hadn't disobeyed God. I was, I believe, exactly where God wanted me for that season. But that's just it. For me, it was only to be *for a season*.

My time working for my local church moulded me, inspired me, grew me, challenged me and matured me, more than I could ever truly articulate, and I'm so grateful for that season. The opportunities I had to overcome challenges, develop strategies and implement ideas were invaluable. The wisdom and leadership I sat under was an incredible privilege. This role permitted me to build on the experiences and knowledge I had gleaned from my *Souled Out* days, and also prepared the way for opportunities still to come.

And yet, throughout my four years on the staff I was given several opportunities to co-lead short-term mission teams, and my heart for overseas mission was stirred again.

Then in 2014, God began to transition me into a new season: one that would indeed lead me overseas. "This is it!" I thought. And off I went to New York City.

I initially signed up for four months in NYC as part of the Metro World Child internship programme but hoped that an opportunity would arise to allow me to stay long-term. As it happens, an opportunity did arise: three opportunities, in fact. Yet my spirit was not at peace with any of them. It didn't make much sense to me at the time, feeling that the "overseas" part of my calling finally had a tick in the box, but I followed God back to Aberdeen nonetheless.

"I'm only back for six months," I assured everyone. "I'll be back in the States by the end of the year." But as month after month passed, I was no closer to returning stateside. Was that it, I wondered, was that my calling to overseas mission fulfilled? Had that been all that God had called me to? Had I waited a decade to receive a four-month stint abroad? I began to spiral. By the end of that first year back in Aberdeen, as I turned twenty-nine years old, feeling dejected and forgotten by God, I hit an all-time low.

What now? Where now? Was it all over? Had my life "peaked" and it was all downhill from here? Had I done something wrong? Had I made the wrong decision? Should I never have left NYC in the first place? Had I just been chasing a fantasy, the romantic idea of "overseas mission", and not really counted the cost of all that it would entail?

The truth is (and it's much easier to see it now in hindsight) that what was to follow would inevitably be some of the most difficult months of my personal and spiritual life to date, yet they proved absolutely essential in the preparation for what was still to come.

Time taught me that those four months in New York City were a dry-run—a dress rehearsal, if you will—for a much greater purpose further down the line. It had been a test of my obedience, a gauge by which to measure my faith and an opportunity for God to reveal himself in new and exciting ways.

Over a decade before, that naïve nineteen-year-old lacked life experience, spiritual disciplines, leadership skills and faith, among (many) other things, to step out back in 2006. But the thirty-year-old me that finally saw the fulfilment of that dream had been shaped and challenged by a number of different roles and relationships, developed spiritual disciplines and deepened her walk with her Father, honed leadership skills in an array of situations and seen countless evidences of God's guidance and provision during that waiting period.

Perhaps you can relate a little to my story, or maybe you have waited longer than I. In fact, it is highly likely you are waiting for something right now: perhaps a promise to be fulfilled, a desire to be met, your partner to return with a fresh cup of coffee . . . Waiting is part of life. Everyone has to wait. It is not something we particularly enjoy doing but it plays a vital part in our life-long adventure with God.

You see, it is in periods of waiting that we learn valuable lessons that will prepare us for what is still to come. Lessons in trusting God to do what he has said he will do. Lessons in releasing promises to God to act in his way and timing, and not interfering ourselves. Waiting is a lesson in trust and obedience. And it can be a very challenging lesson to learn.

Throughout the Bible, men and women of God endured periods of waiting. Some did it well, others . . . not so much.

Abraham and Sarah waited decades for the promised son who would father a nation.

Joseph waited years in a dark prison cell, forgotten by men but not forgotten by God, who promoted him at just the right time.

Anointed as a humble shepherd boy, David spent his twenties being hunted by the jealous king, Saul, waiting for the day he would be crowned himself.

Even Jesus Christ spent thirty years preparing and being prepared for his three-year ministry here on earth.

No-one is exempt from waiting, and very few of us are very good at it. But if we take our God-appointed purpose seriously, we must also learn to welcome and appreciate periods of waiting. Just as when we are faced with challenge, our attitude towards waiting will entirely change our perspective and approach when we consider our circumstances with a kingdom mentality.

I once journaled: "I just don't know what God is calling me to do. He's placed so many dreams in my heart, but I struggle to connect the dots." What I failed to realize at the time was that it was not *my* job to connect the dots. God would do that in time (and he did) in a way that far exceeds anything I could orchestrate myself (and he did that too!).

Often in times of waiting, the future that you once pictured for yourself can begin to look hopeless. But in those moments, we will find that our battle is not against the circumstances themselves, or the time we have to wait: our battle is against hopelessness.

Placing our hope in our own plans, desires or expectations will most often imprison us in hopelessness and defeat. But when our hope rests in our Sovereign Father, it makes waiting all the more bearable. Hope in God (that is, faith), energizes us to keep going; it causes us to charge forward, regardless of the challenges we face. Hope in God never disappoints, because God does not disappoint.

When the Son of God, Jesus Christ, died on the cross, those around him thought that the end had come and that the promise that he would save the world had been lost. Jesus had long foretold of his death and resurrection (John 2:18–22; Matthew 12:39–40), and it had been no secret either:

> The next day, that is, after the day of Preparation, the chief priests and the Pharisees gathered before Pilate and said, "Sir, we remember how that impostor said, while he was still alive, 'After three days I will rise.' Therefore order the tomb to be made secure until the third day, lest his disciples go and steal him away and tell the people, 'He has risen from the dead,' and the last fraud will be worse than the first."
>
> Matthew 27:62-64

The promise had been foretold and, in hindsight, we consider three days not much of a wait at all. But in the meantime? When we are in the midst of waiting, uncertain of what will happen next, it can feel like an eternity, can't it? And that is when our faith is tested the most.

The meantime: a terrible and wonderful thing. We have an intense dislike for the meantime, do we not? On the surface, nothing happens. Nothing exciting or noteworthy, anyway. The media portrays the highlights of a sporting event or music concert, and kindly cuts out the uneventful bits in between. In life, we tend to only share the good bits, the exciting moments that are worth talking about. We don't, ordinarily, share with our friends about how we dressed in the morning, the route we drove to work, or how many loads of laundry we worked our way through at the weekend. Yet these things are all important too, and there is a reason why we do them.

The same is true during periods of waiting. We are far more enthralled by the highlights that occasionally punctuate a season of waiting, highlights that illustrate to us that progress is being made, even when we fail to recognize it in the daily slog. But the daily slog is just as important—more so, even—because without the daily slog we would never have any highlights to share. The daily slog prepares us for those noteworthy moments.

We can also find ourselves cringing in the meantime, embarrassed by our apparent lack of progress or activity. We often make the mistake of taking matters into our own hands and generating activity, just to be seen by others to be doing *something*. Or else we abandon all resolve and just give up, losing sight of the goal that seems to be as far away from us as it has always been. Surely someone, somewhere, dropped the ball on this, because otherwise we would see progress, right?

Well, that depends on where we are looking and upon what our eyes are focused. If we are only looking at the final destination at the end of a long tunnel, we will inevitably get discouraged and want to give up. Hopelessness will defeat us. But if we learn to look for God in the miracles of every day, those small, seemingly insignificant yet God-ordained moments, we will see that progress *is* being made. Every day we grow a little more, mature a little more, learn a little more, understand a little more. Every day that we wait is a little more bearable when we consider the greater purpose, which we are being prepared for, is percolating, unseen. We *are* moving further towards a greater goal or outcome, whatever that may be.

In times of darkness, when confusion, discouragement and doubt threaten to overwhelm us, we need to remind ourselves of God's faithfulness. We need to open our mouths and declare his unfailing goodness, even when we do not see it yet in our own circumstances. When we speak truth and shout praises to the One who loves us more than we could possibly imagine, our focus shifts and we gain a whole new perspective.

The beauty of an adventure is that there is no single, final destination. It is a *journey*. A journey full of twists and turns, never knowing what is just beyond that next corner. When we think of an adventure, we *expect* uncertainty and to wander off the beaten track. So why should life be any different?

The choice is a simple one: wait on God or wish that you had. But this choice is not just a one-off decision made on the day of promise; it is one that we have to make and commit to over and over again. Life is full of periods of waiting, so learning to wait well is a skill that will make every season of life a lot more enjoyable. It may seem like an easy decision to take, but living out that decision when months, or even years, pass can be far more challenging.

In periods of waiting, it can be very hard to "do nothing". Often, the need to do *something* is just so strong. Even those around us—friends and family who know us well—may urge us forward. But if our own desires and the well-intended advice of others contradict the peace in our hearts, we must not allow them to steer us off course. The truth is, we are not called to "do nothing" while we wait. If we use the time correctly, waiting time need not be wasted time but will prove to be invaluable.

A challenge I have faced repeatedly in my journey with God is dealing with uncertainty. I guess none of us can really be certain of what tomorrow will hold, but when God plants dreams and promises in your heart, it feels somewhat harder to wait for the fulfilment of that dream or promise, not knowing when or how it will happen.

I think we find it easier to suffer the time it takes for a personal goal or objective to be realized because we take steps towards it ourselves and the in-between time does not feel so difficult when we are active in our waiting. However, we can be active in our waiting on God's promises too, even if we are to keep our hands off the promise itself.

Let me put it like this: during periods of waiting, do not seek to act on behalf of God. I cringe at the countless times I have tried (and sometimes still try) to give God a "helping hand" to make his promises a reality. However, we all know that God is perfectly capable of fulfilling his purposes all by himself. In this sense, we really should "do nothing". We wait so that we can appreciate that miracles are by the grace of God, and not by anything we can do ourselves.

But, while you leave God to work on his promises to you, you can be working on everything else! Serve, travel, meet new people, study, build friendships, read, delve deeper into God's Word and strengthen your relationship with him. The more you know him, the greater your adventure will be because you will set aside the longing ache for your not-yet-fulfilled promise and begin to enjoy every day as God intended. You will receive fresh perspective to see his hand in every detail, and not just in the milestone moments you so desperately crave.

When we reflect on our lives, we most often focus primarily on the big milestones: a career change, an academic achievement, meeting your spouse, starting a family, moving to a new city. Or perhaps we focus more on the spiritual milestones: accepting Jesus as Lord of our lives, baptism, healing, freedom from a particular sin or addiction. But while we focus on the milestones, God is more interested in the faithful steps in between.

He loves the *process*, more than the destination, because while we watch the changing circumstances around us, he adores watching the internal changes within us.

So why does God ask us to wait? We cannot always be sure, for his ways are far beyond our own comprehension. But it may be because:

- He has lessons to teach us and attitudes to change in us before we can be ready for the next season.
- There are other factors in play that we are blind to (people, opportunities, circumstances) and God uses the time to prepare them and strategically place them for the next season also.
- He wants to see if what we have received on the mountain-top has truly been rooted in our hearts. It is very exciting to receive a word or promise directly from the mouth of God, but there is almost always a delay between the declaration of the promise and the fulfilment of that same promise. God uses that delay to test our faith to see if we really believe that he will do what he has said he will do. How we act in our period of waiting reflects what we truly believe in our hearts.

In that delay, that meantime, that in-between moment, we have choices to make. It is never a one-off decision to wait for the promises of God, but a daily commitment to hope for his best. We choose to wait because:

- We believe that God is true to his Word and will do just as he has said he will do.
- We believe that what God has prepared for us is far beyond anything we could fabricate for ourselves.
- We want to walk in obedience to what God asks us to do and not simply opt for a life of comfort or ease.

But if you are waiting without praying and preparing yourself to receive God's best for you, you are missing the point. Faith without preparation is void and is, therefore, just hope. We will go nowhere if we simply hope things will turn around. Instead, we must believe that they will, pray that they will and prepare ourselves so that we are ready for when they do turn around.

Are you beginning to see the bigger picture? Can you enlarge your vision to see beyond your own, current circumstances? By trusting God, and developing a kingdom-wide panoramic view, we can learn to embrace, value and even *enjoy* periods of waiting (yep, I said it!). When we see the bigger picture, we appreciate that we need the meantime to prepare for future highlights. We recognize that time spent on our knees, in conversation with God and drawing closer to him, will always profit us. We begin to anticipate the stronger, more peaceful "you" that is being developed as we wait. And recognize this: when we journey through those desert moments well, we leave footprints that can lead others safely out too. Nothing is wasted in God's great purpose; he uses every single instance for the greater good.

One of my all-time heroes of the faith is Jim Elliot, an American missionary who was killed, aged just twenty-nine years old, by the very tribe of Ecuadorian Indians he was trying to win for Christ. His journal entries and letters to family members in the years leading up to his death provide evidence of his fierce faith and his desire to do the will of God in his life.

Yet on the face of it, his short life was, for the most part, the "meantime". There were few highlights, as perceived by the world, and some may despair at his death, thinking it to be a premature, tragic loss. But not Jim. Jim saw and celebrated those in-between moments as moments of preparation and communion with his beloved Lord. He faced many times of frustration and impatience, desperate to outwork the vision that God had laid on his heart, but his obedience and commitment to God's way was stronger. He once stated: "Wherever you are, be all there! Live to the hilt every situation you believe to be the will of God."[15] Though Jim's life was short, it was *full*: full of laughter, of deep friendships and of the joy of God.

That day, when Jim and four missionary friends were killed by the Auca Indians, it looked as though the plan had failed, that God's call on Jim's life would not be fulfilled. But God speaks nothing but truth. Proverbs 30:5 assures us that "every word of God proves true; He is a shield to those who take refuge in him."

Less than two years later, Elisabeth Elliot, Jim's wife, along with their daughter Valerie, and the sister of another missionary who had lost his life alongside Jim, moved into the Auca village. Through the love and testimony of these faithful women, many members of the tribe heard about God's love for them and chose to put their trust in him. The vision that God had given Jim for this savage tribe deep in the Ecuadorian jungle became a reality, and Jim had been instrumental in paving the way. He had faithfully played his part and had walked in obedience to all that God had called him to do, rather than always trying to skip ahead, focused on a particular preconceived outcome.

In times of waiting, it can be easy to slip into a dreamlike state where your body is firmly in the present, but your mind and heart have gone ahead and are endeavouring to live prematurely in your promised land. But we must guard our minds and not allow ourselves to drift so far into the future that we miss out on the present. Even while we wait for God's promises, there is a life to be fully embraced and lived out every single day. Be fully present wherever you are right now. It may not be where you want to be, or what you would like to be doing, but when we walk in obedience to where God has placed us at this moment instead of always wishing each day away, we learn to see God in the mundane and life becomes an adventure!

After I returned from NYC to Scotland, I knew I would face a further period of waiting, so I decided that I would embrace every opportunity that came my way (providing it was biblical, of course!). This became one of the best decisions I could have made during that season. Yes, I was still waiting for a greater promise, and it remained in the back of my mind. But that waiting period became fun and enjoyable because as I walked through the door of one opportunity, the next door flew wide open and I embraced the adventure.

God surprised me in so many ways in that season: he reminded me of dormant gifts within me that had not been used for a while; he gave me the honour of ministering to hundreds of people over a period of months; I met new people and allowed him to direct my next steps. Opportunities I could never have imagined were lined up before me, one after the other. He used these opportunities to heal wounds in me and used the people around me to speak words of encouragement and affirmation over me.

I refused to let my doubts, or my fears, or my uncertainty hold me back and keep me "stuck" in my waiting period. Instead of focusing on what I did not yet have, I celebrated what I did have! I invested my time, my gifts and my experience into what was directly before me, and the waiting period felt far less tormenting that it may have done otherwise.

Sometimes we forget to live while we wait, but it is absolutely essential that we do. Life does not wait. It doesn't hit pause until we have everything we are waiting for. For some, waiting can even become an excuse to not do anything at all, to simply "play it safe".

"When I earn enough money, I will . . . "

"Once I am married, I can . . . "

"If I get that promotion, then . . . "

We cannot let waiting become a habit, or we will never live the full and abundant life that God desires for us. He is not some disimpassioned God who wants us to play it safe and just sit, waiting patiently for him. He wants us to take risks, to embrace change and to welcome opportunity as we take every step fully trusting in him.

I believe God speaks promises over us long before he fulfils them for a number of reasons. We can never fully understand the mind of God while we remain here on earth, but the Bible gives us some ideas:

- He proves himself to be faithful. By speaking out a promise in advance, he shows himself to be faithful and true; he shows that his promises are all part of a greater plan, and not some luck that we simply fall into by accident. (See Joshua 23:14, 2 Corinthians 1:20, Hebrews 10:23.)
- He gives us a focus and incentive to be intentional about our preparation. It is much easier to prepare if we have some idea of what we are preparing for. I believe God allows us to glimpse what is up ahead to pique our interest and encourage us to prepare well. (See Psalm 119:49–50, Proverbs 3:5–6, Philippians 1:6.)
- We value the fulfilled promise more when we have had to persevere through the wait, and fight our doubts to receive it. We rarely cherish something that falls quickly into our lap, but when we have invested time, money, energy and tears into something, we appreciate its worth. (See Galatians 6:9, Hebrews 6:11, James 1:12.)

- We seek God more in the wait because we desire the end product, but through that we develop our relationship with God himself. God greatly desires a relationship with us. He longs to speak to us, reveal himself to us and demonstrate his great power. Our wait, our problems, our struggles only encourage us to draw even closer to him. As our relationship with him deepens, the trauma of the wait diminishes and the more equipped we are to maintain that relationship once the promise is fulfilled. (See Matthew 6:33, Acts 17:27, Romans 8:24-28.)

It is as we wait on God that our faith is often tested the most. Who do we truly believe God is? Do we really trust his ways and his timing? Will he come through for us like he has said he will? Through the wait we learn to depend on what God has spoken, and not on the circumstances we see around us. As we wait for the fulfilment of promises, it does us no good to lean on our own understanding.

It can be easy to become discouraged as we wait, but in order to keep moving forward, we must remain focused on who God has called us to be and what he has called us to do. What opportunities are before you in this moment? What gifts and resources can you use to bless others? Resist the temptation to simply stop and wait for the promise; instead continue to sow into all the good things you are currently doing.

You can also begin to prepare yourself today for the vision that God has placed in your heart. Consider what books you could read, what Bible passages you could study and which people you could learn from in order to be that bit wiser, that bit stronger, that bit more prepared. Invest in yourself and in the gifts God has given you, so that when God does call you forward, you are equipped and ready to follow.

Throughout my life there have been many periods of waiting: waiting for change, waiting for opportunities, waiting for the next step forward. But as I reflect on these times, I notice a pattern. The next step was revealed only after I had adjusted my attitude and surrendered my circumstances to God. At first, my prayers were full of angry words, frustrations and asking "why?" It took a long time to realize that I was so busy telling God how unhappy I was that I did not stop to listen and hear his response. But when I surrendered my circumstances to him, he began to move.

One such occasion occurred shortly before I relocated to Germany. I was working in a social outreach project at the time and had initially only agreed to work there for six months, sensing from the start that it was only to be for a short time and that God would call me overseas again. But in my fourth month, I felt a burden to begin a children's ministry in the local community. I did not want to begin something if I was only going to be present for a couple more months, so I committed to a further year in employment: the duration of the next full academic year.

For over a year I lived with a short-term mentality. Every commitment I made had the disclaimer, "If I'm still here, then I will . . . " or, "If I'm not gone by then, perhaps . . . " It was not that I wanted to distance myself from everyone and everything, but rather I did not want to commit to anything I would not see through until the end. But by the following spring, having faced challenges and frustrations both professionally and personally, I decided that living with this short-term mentality was unhelpful for both myself and my colleagues. I stopped using disclaimers and decided to be fully present in the season that God had placed me in.

"OK, God," I said, "if this is where you have me for now, I will be all here. I will stop living in limbo, neither fully in the present, nor fully in the next season. I will resist trying to make the next step happen, so it is up to you to act when that right time comes. I'm committing to 'here' until you move me 'there.'"

I began putting down roots again and, most significantly, decided to put my apartment up for sale. If I was to remain in my home city for the foreseeable future, then I would invest in a larger place that I could be comfortable in.

But a couple of months went by, and my apartment attracted very little interest. A number of people viewed it, there were even some promising conversations about follow-up actions and further negotiation, but it didn't budge.

Yet it was only once my attitude had changed, and I had surrendered to God my desires and expectations about moving overseas, that he began to work. My actions reflected my changed focus and I no longer sought to second-guess God's timetable, but instead to fully embrace my present circumstances. I realized that God had not forgotten me or overlooked me. He had placed me there for that time and with purpose, therefore I was to make best use of my time with those people, in that job, living in that city. My change in attitude changed my whole demeanour, and my remaining months in that season became far more pleasant and enjoyable.

Then, on the last day of that academic year, I flew to Germany to visit a friend for a much-needed weekend break. It was my first time setting foot on German soil (admittedly, a country well down my travel bucket-list), but it was a cheap weekend break and a greatly anticipated reunion with my friend. There was nothing special about the weekend that I had chosen, other than it being the most convenient for each of our schedules, but I also don't believe that it was any accident that it coincided with the last day of that school year. It was there that God began to nudge me forward once again.

My change in attitude had been the catalyst for God to move in me once more. I changed my priorities and how I spent my time; I chose to invest in myself instead of wasting time daydreaming about what I wanted and sulking because I didn't have it yet. I became intentional about my own spiritual growth. I fasted TV and movies that summer (a time-consuming hobby of mine), so that I could better invest that time. I dived into God's Word; I read faith-inspired books packed full of wisdom and personal testimonies. I told God everything that I had been feeling: my hopes, my dreams, my doubts, my disappointments, my failures and my regrets. God reminded me of the purposes he had created me for, but I knew that I was not yet ready to enter into them. Becoming ready became my new goal.

Without rushing ahead or trying to second guess or take control, I simply began asking God, "What next?" And in the meantime, I continued to serve in my existing situation as best as I could.

In the months that followed, God actually used the non-sale of my apartment to direct me further and to finally confirm that a new season was imminent. Though I had initially envisioned this "meantime" season would only last six months, it did, in fact, last a little over two years. But the growth and preparation I experienced in that time was absolutely essential in allowing me to step into all that God had prepared for me in Germany. I am unspeakably grateful for that meantime.

During that period of waiting, there were certainly moments when I became disillusioned by my circumstances. But if we forget what we are waiting for and we forget the One who promised it, we will inevitably begin to search for our own solutions. Instead, we need to allow conviction and truth to guide us, even if our emotions take longer to catch up. We need to allow God's voice and the peace that he gives to be our compass through the meantime.

Over the past fifteen years, my understanding of God's promises has changed significantly. I once believed that God would act immediately after he had declared a promise, and when circumstances only partly matched what he had declared, I assumed I had misunderstood or misheard. Essentially, I adjusted the promise to fit the circumstances, instead of waiting for the circumstances to catch up to the promise. I found myself believing that, as I stepped into a full-time ministry role, God's promises for my life had been fulfilled—at the tender age of twenty-three. Oh, how wrong I was!

As my journey through life has twisted and turned since then, I have learnt that God speaks the truth, the whole truth and nothing but the truth. Yes, there are times when we perhaps misunderstand what God has declared, or we squeeze his words into a mould of our own desires or schedule, but what he says cannot and will not fail. If he says he will do something, you can be assured he will do it. In his own way, and in his own time.

Don't be deceived, either, thinking that God has only one promise for your life. That is simply not true. Consider Abraham. God promised Abraham, in Genesis 12, that he would bless Abraham with a great family, through whom he would spawn the Israelite nation: God's chosen people. Abraham's descendants would also include King David, and Jesus Christ himself.

But there was only one problem. Sarah, Abraham's wife, was barren. Years passed, decades even, and still they were unable to conceive. They waited, and they waited. How could Abraham possibly father a nation if he and his wife were unable to have children?

As they grew older and the likelihood of seeing God's promise fulfilled grew faint, they took matters into their own hands. Sarah presented her own slave woman, Hagar, to her husband and suggested that they might have a child through her instead. And here's the crunch: "And Abram [Abraham] listened to the voice of Sarai [Sarah]" (Genesis 16:2b).

Suggestions like this, perhaps once considered laughable, can begin to draw appeal the longer we wait, when we begin to feel that God has forgotten about us and his promises to us. If Abraham had only listened to the voice of God, he would have avoided the adultery he was about to enter into. But in that moment of weakness and frustration, tired of waiting for the fulfilment of God's promise, he listened to the voice of his wife, who had sought to find a solution—to "join the dots", if you will—her own way.

Inevitably, nine months later a boy was born to Abraham and Hagar, and they named him Ishmael. Abraham was now eighty-six years old, yet Ishmael was not the fulfilment of God's promise to him.

As Abraham approached his centennial birthday, God reiterated his promise to Abraham:

> Behold, my covenant is with you, and you *shall* be the father of a multitude of nations. . . . I will make you exceedingly fruitful, and I will make you into nations, and kings shall come from you. And I will establish my covenant between me and you and your offspring after you throughout their generations for an everlasting covenant, to be God to you and to your offspring after you. And I will give to you and to your offspring after you the land of your sojournings, all the land of Canaan, for an everlasting possession, and I will be their God.
>
> *Genesis 17:4–8 (emphasis added)*

But *how*? How was this possible, with Abraham and Sarah both nearly a hundred years old and long past child-bearing years? Only God. Only *God* could make his promise a reality. That is exclusively how God's promises work: they are impossible without him. But that's the best part!

Nearly thirty years after God's promise to Abraham, Sarah conceived (a human impossibility in her old age), and she gave birth to Isaac. Through Isaac, the promised son, the greater promise of the Israelite nation would be fulfilled. And through this birth line, the Son of God would be born as a man, the long-promised Messiah, to save the world.

This was God's plan all along. He hadn't forgotten; he hadn't messed up; he didn't need to come up with a Plan B because he had missed his window of opportunity. God knew exactly what he was doing.

Abraham and Sarah waited a long time to see their promise. In fact, they never really did see the entire promise fulfilled, for it was a promise that would be outworked in generations to come. Yet God did exactly what he said he would do. Along the way, he spoke other promises over their lives—the promise of a son, of a land, of numerous descendants—all significant steps towards a much greater purpose.

You may still be waiting to see that big God-given dream realized, but I can guarantee he is speaking smaller promises and working smaller miracles in your life, all in preparation for what is still to come. In 2013, I journaled: "I'm not 100% sure what God is calling me to yet, but I now realize that I don't need to be 100% sure. I only need to trust God and follow his individual steps rather than trying to guess the end result and make my own way there."

You see, there is fun and adventure and joy to be had on the journey too, not just in the end result. Don't you enjoy the anticipation of wrapping a gift for a family member, excited to see the look on their face when they rip off the paper? Or the thrill of boarding a flight to a far-off destination for a much-needed break? The journey is much easier on the way there than on the way back, am I right?

What if *every* day was lived in great anticipation? Anticipation of what God is going to do today, of how he might act on your behalf, or what he might whisper into your heart? Are you paying attention to his work in the journey, or are you only waiting impatiently for the outcome?

The Israelites, the ancestral nation of Abraham, would one day enter into the promised land that God had set aside for them. However, their journey was anything but simple.

We have already considered how unlikely it seemed that a nation could spawn from Abraham in the first place. Then, after Isaac came Jacob; Jacob, otherwise known as Israel, fathered the Twelve Tribes which eventually compiled the nation of Israel.

We then pick up the plight of the Israelites in Exodus, when God's chosen people are so great in number that Pharaoh, the King of Egypt, fears they will rise up against him, so he enslaves them. But God had not forgotten his people. He raised up Moses, an Israelite himself, to advocate for the Israelite nation and lead them safely out of Egypt to the land that had been promised to Abraham several hundred years earlier.

Exodus 13:17–18 reads: "When Pharaoh let the people go, God did not lead them by way of the land of the Philistines, although that was near. For God said, 'Lest the people change their minds when they see war and return to Egypt.' But God led the people around by the way of the wilderness towards the Red Sea. And the people of Israel went up out of the land of Egypt equipped for battle."

God led his people on a *roundabout* way. It wasn't the quickest route, or the most direct, but he had a reason to do this: to prepare them for what they were yet to face. He cared for them too much to allow them to enter the wilderness without readying them for battle first. He knew what they would face on their journey to the promised land and he did not want anything to cause them to miss out on the great gift he wanted to give them. God was more concerned about their readiness than sticking to a particular schedule.

And is that not true for us, too? God rarely takes us on the quickest, easiest or most direct route to our promised land; his timetable is more often dictated by our readiness, availability and obedience.

The Israelites wandered the desert for forty years, but the distance they covered should only have taken them eleven days (Deuteronomy 1:2–3). So, why the delay? Because they were not yet ready to enter into their promised land. Time after time, they failed to trust God; they disobeyed God's commands spoken through Moses, and they complained a whole lot. They were so distracted by their existing circumstances that they failed to see with faith what was still ahead of them. They forgot what they were waiting for.

But God knew that if the Israelites could not trust him in the desert, when things were tough and their own abilities could only take them so far, then they would not depend on him in the promised land either. And we face exactly the same challenge. Until we learn to trust God in good times as well as bad, we will remain in a season of waiting. It is not to punish us, or discourage us, but because God loves us too much to allow us to face situations we are not yet ready for. He uses times of waiting to draw us closer to himself.

Before stepping into full-time ministry, I was a high school physics teacher. I absolutely loved teaching. It brought me such joy to see my students engage with what I was teaching and show an interest in my subject. My favourite time of the year, however, was the end of year exams. (I know, I know, I sound like I take great delight in the stress of children . . . but that is not why it was my favourite time, honest!) I liked these few weeks the best because I got to watch my students truly apply themselves as the exams approached. Those who had fooled around all year and taken a somewhat aloof approach to the class were now shaken into paying attention and desperately sought my help at every available opportunity.

I remember two boys in particular. They were a comedy duo; you never got one without the other. They were best friends and the class clowns in one of my fourth-year classes. This particular class was hard work. The structure of the timetable that year had meant that, for these students, physics had been the most favourable option in a selection of unpopular subjects. For the most part, they were disinterested in the subject and, therefore, disengaged.

As their physics exam approached, these two boys asked if they could spend their free periods in my classroom, working through old exam papers for practice. Naturally, I agreed. One such period, they came in with a look of great confusion on their faces because there was a particular topic that had them baffled. No matter how much they had tried to figure it out for themselves, they concluded that they needed my help. Step by step, I took them through a practice exam question, using it to illustrate the misunderstood topic, until that dreamy look of comprehension dawned on their faces. That look, *that* moment, was why I became a teacher: to bring someone from a place of confusion and frustration into the euphoria and peace of understanding.

I can only imagine that God looks on us a little like that too. In seasons of waiting, perhaps we take the role of the class clown and fail to pay much attention to what God is trying to teach us. Maybe we resent being there because we would not choose to be there if we had a better alternative. But when we accept that this is the journey we are on and that God is using it to teach us, we often find that the waiting season need not be drawn out. He longs for us to come to him with questions and frustrations so that he can help eradicate the confusion and bring us into peace. He may not provide all the answers, but he will journey with us to bring us into a better understanding and a better perspective. He, too, longs to see the dreamy look of comprehension on our faces when we look back and see evidence that he has been guiding us all along.

I have waited for many things: hopes, dreams, promises, desires. And as I have waited, God has asked me to do things that I was less than enthusiastic about participating in. They were not the roles, responsibilities, jobs, situations I wanted to find myself in, and I resented them. But, whether I liked it or not, these circumstances were at the centre of God's plan for my life in that season.

It can be so tempting to look for something better, can't it? At least, what *we* think will be better. But being obedient and living in the season and circumstances that God has called us to is actually the best place we could possibly be, even if we don't appreciate it right away.

Knowing you have been obedient to God brings with it strength and determination to just keep going. Bad days are made better by the conviction that you have obeyed God. You hold on just a little longer when you face weeks so bad that you just want to give up, because you cling to the knowledge that God is using it to prepare you for what is still to come.

When we persevere through those tough periods of apparent stagnation, God offers glimpses of his work behind the scenes. He helps us find joy in our hidden acts of service. He uses us to encourage others as they learn from our own struggles.

In that two-year interlude before God called me to Germany, I waited on him to show me my next step; while trying to remain in the present, my heart yearned for all that was still to come. One night, I scribbled this prayer in my journal:

> God, I pray you would protect my mind from over-analysing or trying to figure out what you are doing. Instead, help me to enjoy the ride! Help me to not be so focused on the future that I miss the present. God, I pray for wisdom and discernment as I seek to identify and develop my unique role in your church body. I pray once again for clarity in direction, and I pray, God, that you would

open the right doors for me. I believe the right opportunities will present themselves to me and you will give me a peace about them. God, I believe you have the perfect role for me—one that is fun, challenging, rewarding, too good to be true. God help me to find that role, grab it with two hands, and commit to it long-term, so that I can invest in people and see them grow. And God, in this waiting time, in this time of uncertainty, I pray you would help me use my time wisely and prioritize good things—people, time with you, time of reflection and prayer—so that I can be ready for what comes next. Thank you for the journey you have taken me on so far . . .

At the end of that year, more than nine months after I prayed that prayer, my colleague pointed out that, despite my feelings, frustrations and disappointments, I had walked in obedience to God that year. On the face of it, it felt like an uneventful year, but it was encouraging to be reminded that, in spite of my own feelings, I had obeyed God.

We may be waiting for God to show us the next step, when all he asks of us in this moment is to continue doing what he last asked us to do. It is always easier to ride out the tough seasons—whether they be stormy or seemingly endless—when we know we are in the place God wants us to be. If God led you here, you can trust him to lead you out again, in his way and in his timing. But while you wait, be all you can be: try new things, build godly relationships, be all there. Do not look back on this season with regrets, wishing you had *enjoyed* each day, and not just tolerated them.

Resist forfeiting your promised land for the "easier road" just because the wait, the lesson, the unknown is hard. Don't disregard the promises of God from years ago just because they have not yet been fulfilled. God's best is always worth the wait.

Do you think the disciples would have acted as they did if they had known how little time they would have with Jesus? Do you think they would have fallen asleep on the night Jesus was arrested instead of praying in the Garden of Gethsemane, as Christ had asked them to? Preparation time is a gift, and we need to be careful not to waste it.

After my ten-year wait for the mission field, I had the wisdom to see that God's call on my life was no romantic fantasy. To be able to share such incredible testimonies, I knew I must first face incredible challenges. It took every lesson God had taught me in that decade of waiting to navigate my initial step to move to Germany. Every relational chip and bruise that I had suffered historically helped me to show compassion to those I would later meet and work with. Every previously answered prayer inspired me to raise my hands once more and trust God to meet each need. Every past mistake and failing reminded me to lean on God even more heavily in every uncertainty.

Only after ten years did I understand that I didn't (and still don't) have what it takes to fulfil God's call on my life. I wonder to myself, "Why me? Why choose me, God?" But all God is really looking for in each of us is the willingness to obey him. I may not be able to *fulfil* his call, but I can *answer* it. I can walk the path *with* him. I trust my Sovereign God and I believe that he knows what he's doing. Therefore I continue to step out in faith and in obedience to him, thanking him for the ten-year wait, for the way he prepared me and for all that he taught me along the way.

The Bible assures us that those who wait on the Lord will not be put to shame (Isaiah 49:23). God will not let us down, or make us look like fools by leaving us to wait indefinitely for a promise that will never come; that is not in his nature. He rejoices over those who walk in his ways and trust him to come through for them. He will make heroes of those who wait for his best and do not take matters into their own hands. Be strong. Let your heart take courage, and wait for the Lord.

It doesn't matter how equipped or ready we feel, God knows best. Trust his ways. Trust his timing. Get busy investing in yourself during this time of waiting, and not just impatiently willing it to pass. Then be ready to obey him when he speaks. There's no greater adventure than a life with God holding the map.

The ultimate goal, however, is not to see promises or desires fulfilled, but to be moulded into the image of Christ: "Therefore be imitators of God, as beloved children. And walk in love, as Christ loved us and gave himself up for us, a fragrant offering and sacrifice to God" (Ephesians 5:1–2). That is the big picture. That is the ultimate goal. That is what we are all actively waiting for.

8

Anticipating Adventure

New York City: the place where dreams come true! Or so they say. And it had, indeed, always been a dream of mine to visit. I longed to see the bright lights, sense the electric atmosphere and drink in the multicultural flavours available on every street corner.

For me, to visit New York City felt like a dream, an impossibility. I always imagined that I would be much older (and earning far more money!) before I visited the city, so it had never even crossed my mind to consider it as a holiday destination in my early twenties. However, one Saturday afternoon, over a Starbucks coffee date, my friend told me she hoped to visit NYC later that year and, for the very first time, the possibility of making my dream a reality flitted through my mind.

The truth was, NYC was more than just a once-in-a-lifetime holiday destination to me. The longing to visit stirred something deeper within me, and that stirring later nudged me into taking the plunge, that is, spending more than I would normally spend on a holiday to accompany my friend on a five-day break in the Big Apple in September 2012. Surprisingly (and yet not surprising at all), I experienced a sense of familiarity and ease from the moment I landed at JFK airport. Despite having never visited the city before, it instantly felt like home.

For a further two years, my spirit continued to yearn for NYC. It seemed like such an unlikely goal, but I could not shake the feeling that I wasn't done with the city yet.

In those uncertain months, I began to relate well to the story in Mark 4:35–41. It recounts a time when Jesus and his disciples faced a huge storm. Jesus had spent the entire day teaching and using parables to illustrate the gospel message, then, declaring "Let us go across to the other side", he and his companions hopped into a boat to cross the Sea of Galilee.

Jesus, exhausted from a long day of speaking to the crowds, fell asleep, but a great storm arose on the sea, battering the boat with large waves and strong winds. Terrified, his disciples woke Jesus and cried, "Teacher, do you not care that we are perishing?"

Immediately, Jesus commanded the wind and waves to cease and the storm obeyed, restoring calm instantaneously. He asked them, "Why are you so afraid? Have you still no faith?"

The disciples had been faced with a crisis and feared for their lives, so their natural response was fear. Many of us may not have faced death, but, no doubt, we can all remember crisis moments in our lives when we were overwhelmed by the stormy circumstances raging around us and we responded in fear, uncertain that God was really in control.

But the disciples' fear, like ours, was misplaced. Before they climbed into the boat, Jesus had declared that they were going to *the other side* (not that they would go to the middle and drown!). If the disciples had truly understood who Jesus was, they would have feared him far more than the storm and would have been assured that they really were going to *the other side*.

Yet they had missed the memo. They had not fully appreciated that Jesus was God incarnate. They accepted his declaration merely as a good intention, and not as indisputable hard fact.

Do we react to God's proclamations over our own lives like this too? Do we hear only good intentions when God states them as truth? Do we respond in fear, despair and doubt when the storm rises up around us, instead of reminding ourselves who travels in the boat alongside us?

"Let's go to the other side." This declaration pursued me for months during that two-year wait, and became the promise I clung to when the wind and waves of life threatened to steal it away. I believed God had said we (he and I) would go to the other side (of the Atlantic Ocean) and, though it seemed an impossible dream, I chose to trust his Word and anticipate the fulfilled promise.

Through the storm, God continued to prepare me for the next season, though I had little idea of what it might look like. I began to gently push at doors of opportunity, but I was also careful not to try to make things happen on my own.

My journal entries in 2014 catalogue the events of what would become a very significant season, full of lessons and of God's guidance and provision:

> 26 January 2014: Today's devotional reading, plus a conversation with a friend, has encouraged me to take the step to pursue a trip to NYC this year. I've been putting it off, mainly for financial reasons, but also for fear of what others may think. But I believe this is a step I could take and will trust that God will make the way clear, and perhaps use this to show me more of where he is leading me.

Convinced that God had a plan for me in NYC that would unfold later that year, I sold my car to fund ten days in NYC plus a five-day break with friends in Los Angeles. My time in New York was to be split between a few days alone in Manhattan to explore, read and pray, plus a week at Metro World Child's taster programme, MWC Bootcamp.

The idea of visiting Metro World Child had also been an idea that had danced through my mind for those two years, but it had never quite felt right ... until then. I knew a number of people who had worked or visited there before, and I deliberated over whether or not I should too. But what was one week if it turned out it wasn't the right place for me? I decided to give it a go.

> 23 February 2014: I booked my flights to NYC / Metro / LA this week but, now that it's done, I've grown anxious about going alone, about being disappointed following such great expectations, and about what others might think.

Notice I was concerned about what others could think of my actions. I recall thinking that NYC was not considered to be your typical mission field; it was no African orphanage or Balkan refugee camp. It, perhaps, seemed too easy to fly to the glitz and glam of Manhattan and call it "mission". But every city, town and village in the world has someone who needs to hear about Jesus. It should not be a question of where *we* want to go, but where God is leading us to.

After applying for Bootcamp, I began to read the autobiography of Bill Wilson, Founder and Pastor of Metro World Child, entitled *Whose Child is This?*, to gain a better understanding of what I would be involved with for the week and the challenges that I might face. I can be easily distracted at times, so it sometimes takes me weeks, if not months, to finish reading a book. This one, however, I worked through in just six days. I couldn't put it down! It became instrumental in that season in aligning me with God's purposes for what was still to come. I recall hearing a church leader once state that it is not the content of a book that is significant, but the season in which you read it. This was glaringly evident for me in that moment.

My heart echoed the words that I read in Pastor Bill's book:

> Even though the program [I was involved with] was a huge success, there was a restlessness in my spirit. I knew that God had something else on my agenda. I didn't know where it was or what it was, but my heart was open. I always wanted to do more and believed I could.[16]

Having booked MWC Bootcamp to push at a door of opportunity, God used a series of events to then confirm that the MWC three-month internship was to be my next step.

> 22 April 2014: Interestingly, over the last couple of days I've been wondering if I should do the Metro internship for three months at the end of this year . . . I was thinking through this very thing (worrying over financing it!) when my colleague sitting across from me in the church office, completely out of the blue, suggested I do an internship in the US for three months! She said she didn't know where the thought had come from; "perhaps it was a God thing!"

By the time I was ready to fly to New York for Bootcamp, I had been accepted onto the internship, shared my plans with my family and close friends, and submitted my resignation at work. God may ask us to wait and take his time preparing us, but when he acts, he often acts quickly!

> 29 May 2014: (On flight to MWC Bootcamp) Today I'm feeling a lot more uneasy—anxious, lonely, distracted—than I expected. I think more than anything I'm worried that the reality of NYC / Metro won't live up to my expectations. But I need to remember that when God directs my path, I won't be disappointed.

> 2 June 2014: While I've felt at home during the day, fear comes at night, and I worry I don't have what it takes to stay here. Only yesterday, two kids were stabbed, one died, in Brooklyn. Can I hear, see, witness, experience things like this and still sleep at night? I don't want to start this if I can't finish it, but it terrifies me!

Fear became a very real battle for me while I was there: fear like I had never experienced before. The stories I had read in *Whose Child is This?*—of violence, drugs, rape and murder—played heavily on my mind and I sincerely doubted that I could or should still participate in the internship.

As I sat in the back of one of the signature yellow Yogi Bear trucks one balmy evening after Bootcamp, having spent the day in the Bronx visiting families living in the Projects, I prayed. I spent the hour-long journey back to the ministry's headquarters holding back the tears and silently pouring my heart out to God. It felt somewhat like a negotiation; I began by stating all my fears, worries and concerns. Then I shared my doubts, my weaknesses, my feelings of inadequacy. I told him what I needed from him if we were going to do this, and do this *together*. But I ended the turbulent prayer with surrender: if this truly was what God had called me to do (and I knew that it was), then I would be obedient, even though every part of me in that moment wanted desperately to leave and never return.

God, in his goodness and grace, led me to the passage in Acts, when God spoke to the apostle Paul and encouraged him to continue doing as he was doing, despite opposition. He said, "Don't be afraid! Speak out! Don't be silent! For I am with you, and no-one will attack and harm you, for many people in this city belong to me" (Acts 18:9–10, NLT).

These verses held so much promise for me: promise of his protection, promise of his presence, and promise of his purpose which was to use me, to speak through me, and to win souls for Christ through my obedience. These verses anchored me for the next six months, repeating them to myself often in moments when fear threatened to defeat me.

> 7 June 2014: On our way home from the pizza place this evening, we saw a guy pull a gun on someone else. However, it later turned out to be an undercover cop. It was nerve-wracking, but I didn't panic, which I think is testament to the growth in me this week.

By the end of those ten days in NYC, my heart had done a 360-degree turn. Through excitement to apprehension to fear to anticipation, God used the Bootcamp to give me a glimpse of what was to come, but he also used it to show me that I was not alone; we were going to do this *together*. I would never have lasted the full duration of the internship if I had not used every ounce of resolve I had to lean on him and draw courage from him on a daily basis.

This resolve was necessary when I considered my finances, too. One of the reasons I had taken so long to visit NYC in the first place was because flights alone were just too pricey. But having committed to the internship, I now had three-months' living expenses to fund on top of that.

As I prayed and pondered over this very issue, I thought of Jesus' reminder to us in Matthew 6 that we have no reason to worry about what we will eat or wear, or how our needs will be met. Birds do not plant or reap, or store up rations for themselves, yet God still provides for them when they are in need. So, if he'll do that for some of the smallest and most insignificant creatures on the planet, will he not meet our needs too?

With less than a month to go before I left for the internship, God provided what I needed—$3000—in the space of just one weekend. I have faced a number of financially challenging moments throughout my faith adventure thus far, but this, and other testimonies I have witnessed along the way, always build my faith to wait for and receive the next miracle.

After two years of God declaring that he would take me to the other side, he did. He led me there, he provided for me there, he guided me while I was there, and he used the experience to open my eyes to the reality of New York City living. I witnessed not only the glamorous minority in Manhattan and the trendy artists who dwell in hipster corners of Brooklyn, but the large single-parent families who live in rundown one-bedroom apartments in Harlem and the Bronx. I became a friend for the lonely, I embodied safety for those who lived in fear and I embraced those who were desperately deprived of love.

I was so naive when I arrived on the other side. I recall my first night there; I was standing speaking to the Intern Coordinator and heard a series of bangs and cracks outside. "Ooo, fireworks!" I exclaimed, just looking for something to say to break the awkward silence.

"Erm, no . . . " she said, with a mixed look of surprise and concern, "that's gun shots."

The internship ended mid-December, and I headed back to Scotland to spend Christmas with my family. But in my heart I carried many questions surrounding what came next:

> 28 December 2014: I've realized that the supernatural boldness I leant on in NYC has gone (or was subjective, or maybe I've disregarded it) since I got back. I've been fearful about stupid things and have been coasting along on the faith and trust I had in the lead-up to, and during, Metro. But now I need to refocus my eyes and fix them on Jesus (in him I need have NO fear) and seek him for direction, purpose and promises fulfilled in this new season.

It became so evident to me, as I readjusted to life back in Scotland, that I found it much easier to trust God when "on mission" than when faced with "normal life". Quitting my job, going to the other side of the world for three months, generating no income and doing it alone was easier to do than returning home where, arguably, I had a home, a couple of job prospects and a host of friends and family members around me. I wrongly assumed that the responsibility of what happened next fell on *my* shoulders, because the possibilities were *tangible*. When there are no doors to push at, we have no option but to trust God, because there is literally nothing we *can* do ourselves. But when faced with multiple opportunities, the decision of choosing which one to follow became overwhelming.

Why was I overwhelmed? Because, once again, I was fearful. This time, I was fearful of making the wrong decision and not walking in God's best for me. But our Heavenly Father doesn't just leave us to sink or swim, he graciously walks with us step by step. Moments of waiting may rattle us a bit, but we will not miss the will of God if we are truly seeking the will of God.

> 30 December 2014: One of the reasons I chose to do the internship was because I didn't feel like I was making much of a difference while working "behind the scenes" in ministry, but interestingly I feel the same way when "on the front line", so I guess it's a mentality shift I need; I need to believe that any work for the kingdom will reap a harvest. I need to work to my strengths (behind the scenes) while not losing the rawness of the front line.

I have already touched on this in a previous chapter but, for me, this was a huge lesson. I had got caught up in comparing myself to others and missing the fact that God uses us in different ways and places us in different situations because we all have a specific part to play. There is no ranking system of what work is more "godly"; the work is godly when it is assigned by God himself and we obediently accept. Though this lesson felt a little like a reprimand, I was so grateful for God's grace in teaching me this lesson and using the experience to remind me of the value and worth he has already placed on me and the gifts he personally chose to give to me.

Months and months of reflection and praying were required to fully process and appreciate my time in NYC. I had left as one person and returned as another, and that is no small thing. Everyone, myself included, wrongly assumed that I would—and could—just slot back into what had been my norm before I left. But I no longer fitted there. Yet where did I fit? My eyes had been opened, my perspective and focus had shifted, the yearning in my heart to be a world-changer had grown, but

I felt increasingly out of place, not knowing just where "my" place was. I thought it was still in New York . . .

> 21 February 2015: I have been pushing on NYC doors this week but getting nowhere. Two opportunities seemed exciting at first glance, but I had no peace while exploring the possibilities further . . . I'm frustrated that I don't know what the specifics of my calling are—I want to help people and point them to Jesus. But where, how and with whom, I do not know.

In Acts 16 we read about the Apostle Paul's second missionary journey. The book's author, Luke, writes about how Paul and his companions were "forbidden by the Holy Spirit to speak the word in Asia" and "they attempted to go into Bithynia, but the Spirit of Jesus did not allow them" (Acts 16:6–7). Then, "a vision appeared to Paul in the night: a man of Macedonia was standing there, urging him and saying, 'Come over to Macedonia and help us.' And when Paul had seen the vision, immediately we sought to go on into Macedonia, concluding that God had called us to preach the gospel to them" (Acts 16:9–10). These verses describe how God guided the men and illustrate to us how closed doors of opportunity are as important as open ones. God uses both to steer us and guide us on this great adventure. Our intentions may be good and honourable, but if it is not God's best for us, he will kindly stand in our path. But God is no puppet-master either; he allows us free will and if we choose to ignore his gentle steer, he will sadly allow us to walk right by him. Yet when we seek his best, he gladly protects us from anything less than extraordinary!

Perhaps redirection will not come immediately. Perhaps we will have to remain in the hallway just a little longer. But when we keep our eyes open and our ears alert to God's voice, we will soon see the right door standing ajar, and with faith we can walk through it. Sometimes we would never have made it to the right place if it were not for closed doors stopping us from reaching the wrong places. What may feel like disappointment at the time is actually paving the way for something much greater.

It took a further nine months for me to finally accept that the NYC season was over. God had indeed taken me to the other side, but the season was considerably shorter than I had expected that it would be. Yet my anticipation for the next season grew, now that I believed and understood that God would be true to his Word, and if he spoke something over me, it was *guaranteed* to come to pass. God taught me many things during that two-year NYC season, but most of all he proved his faithfulness, his protection, his provision and his timing.

I began to consider other promises God had declared over my life in the past: things he wanted me to do, or places he wanted me to go. I remembered the crazy dreams he had planted in my heart and the unlikelihood of those dreams becoming a reality. And yet . . . had he not just proved that he is true to his Word? Had he not just fulfilled one of those impossible dreams of ministering in "the greatest city on earth"?

From the very beginning, God has been a God of truth. Every time Genesis 1 records "God said . . . ", it always happens, just as he has said. What he speaks, will be. It *will* be. It is not just a suggestion, or an intention, but a fact. When God speaks something over your life, claim it! Believe it! Remind yourself of it, even when circumstances would suggest otherwise. Because when God declares a promise over you, nothing will satisfy you until it is fulfilled.

Don't forget the promises that God once whispered into your heart. Don't think that you have missed your opportunity. Don't consider yourself not good enough, not holy enough, not young enough, not old enough, not . . . whatever lies are swirling around your head. Wait. Wait well. Wait with anticipation. Wait with intention. Prepare. Allow yourself to be prepared. And at God's appointed time, be ready to just say "yes".

Resist, too, misreading a delayed response to be a "no" response. We all have many tasks and roles that God wishes us to fulfil in his name. Every season, every mountain-top experience, every struggle in the valley is shaping us and preparing us for all that God has for us. There is no "peak" until we reach heaven. God *always* has more.

When our heart is stirred, it reminds us not to settle or become complacent with our current circumstances; instead, it prompts us to continue pressing into him and all that he has for us. There are times when God calls us and plants us somewhere for long seasons; we invest in something and journey with those people, that ministry, that local church. But there are also shorter seasons—middle moments—when God intends for us to only remain there a short time. The challenge, of course, is identifying the difference, and not using difficulty or discontentedness as a reason to run away. Our approach to either season should be the same: to remain there until God calls us onwards.

Fortunately, the fulfilment of God's purposes and promises in our lives is dependent on *his* faithfulness, not ours. And what a relief that should be to us! We are but fallible creatures that make mistakes, no matter how determined we are to walk in his ways. But the good news is that God knows this about us and wishes to partner with us anyway. He does not expect us to (or want us to) walk this journey alone. Indeed, it is impossible for us to reach our full potential without his help. Our effectiveness in doing the will of God is less about our own efforts, and more about how much we depend on him.

When we anticipate God's leading in our lives, we often respond in one of two ways. Either we dive headfirst into an opportunity and find ourselves rushing ahead of him, or we become overwhelmed and run in the opposite direction.

When we move too quickly, we try to take matters into our own hands, fitting mismatched pieces of the jigsaw awkwardly together in an effort to reach where we perceive the destination to be. We recognize needs and endeavour to plan and strategize to find solutions ourselves, instead of trusting God to provide in the best and most timely way. The danger is, of course, that when we fail to find solutions ourselves, fear and doubt creep in.

I have long given up on trying to mentally compute and understand what God is doing in my life. I previously depended on my own skills in troubleshooting and problem solving to seek to comprehend the intricacies of God's careful work in every detail and circumstance, yet when my human mind could not comprehend these circumstances, fear and doubt descended upon me. I would doubt my ability to hear and understand God's voice, or fear that I had missed a step somewhere. But Isaiah 55:8–9 reminds us that, "my thoughts are not your thoughts, neither are your ways my ways, declares the Lord. For as the heavens are higher than the earth, so are my ways higher than your ways and my thoughts than your thoughts." God will often grant us limited insight if we are prepared to receive it, but we will never fully understand why he speaks and acts and positions and permits the way that he does. Instead, our deep desire to comprehend must be replaced by an even deeper conviction to simply trust. Do we trust that God is at the centre of our circumstances? Do we believe that he is up to something much bigger, even if we don't have the faintest idea what that "something" is?

When our hearts are inclined to seek and do the will of God, he is faithful in showing us the way to go. He *wants* to participate in adventure with us. He *wants* to surprise us and demonstrate his miraculous power. Therefore he is not going to let us miss his careful leading. It may not come in a pillar of cloud by day and a pillar of fire by night, like the Israelites experienced in their journey to the promised land, but I believe it will be just as apparent and certain.

God uses many ways to speak to his people: some obvious and others, less so. But he knows who he is talking to and will tailor his direction to the one who is meant to hear it. What is a clear signpost for you may mean nothing to another, but God's guidance works hand-in-hand with our internal spiritual navigation system, the Holy Spirit. When God speaks and directs, the Holy Spirit within us leaps to respond. Our conviction—that deep, internal, unwavering certainty that God has spoken—is the secret to living our God-led adventure. It is this voice that steers us through all of life's challenges and decisions, seeking to keep us on the path God has placed before us.

At times we doubt we can sense his gentle hand, because, in fact, his will is for us to stand still for a time and not to move forward or backward, to the left or to the right. But God's call to stand still for a time is just as significant as moving in the direction he points us in.

In his journals, Jim Elliot put it this way:

> He will lead you and not let you miss your signs. Rest in this—it is his business to lead, command, impel, send, call, or whatever you want to call it. It is your business to obey, follow, move, respond, or what have you ... The sound of 'gentle stillness' after all the thunder and wind have passed will be the ultimate word from God.[17]

God's voice is persistent; it chases us with purpose and longing. It is the thought that you just can't shake, the idea that seems far beyond anything you could have dreamt up yourself. It is the cause that keeps you up at night, knowing you won't rest until something is done about it. You may not understand where, when or how you can make a difference, but there is no doubt in your mind that you will act. That you *must* act. "Now when these signs meet you, do what your hand finds to do, for God is with you" (1 Samuel 10:7).

That is where faith begins its play. Faith is lived out one step at a time. Faith is required for you to act after conviction has told you what to do. We do not know where faith is taking us or what will happen, but we follow, not because we trust ourselves, but because we trust the One who is leading.

I talk often about "open doors", and these opportunities have sometimes been very normal, everyday chances to help someone, to take a step forward in my career or ministry, or to visit and be inspired by a new city. But other "open doors" have been incredible opportunities that I could never have expected or planned for myself. They are once-in-a-lifetime events that simply cannot be passed up. The one thing they all have in common, however, is the fact that God has cleared a path across these thresholds. My job was to simply walk through them.

However, *closed* doors are a blessing too. When things don't quite work out the way we had hoped or, try as you might, there are just too many challenges to overcome, these doors swing shut and we are sometimes left feeling discouraged or defeated. But, when we earnestly seek God's best for our lives, he will use closed doors to protect us, redirect us and ultimately make way for something far greater. His denial of our own desires is *always* done out of love. We may not understand or appreciate his actions at the time, but when we learn to trust him, we surrender all of our wants, our expectations and our uncertainty too.

Yet, there are times when we may think we know better. I did, not long after I moved to Germany. I had relocated there (stepping through a wide-open door) and had settled into language school (another wide-open door). After only a couple of weeks in the country, I applied for, interviewed for, and was successfully offered a job. I could not believe how easy the process had been! Yet something inside of me niggled and began to make me feel uneasy about the whole thing.... By the end of my first day of training, and having read through the terms of my contract in full, I knew in my spirit that it was not an open door, so I respectfully informed my nearly-new employer that I was no longer interested, and that was the end of that.

But I continued to keep an eye out for work. Except that, when I prayed about work, God reassured me there was no need for me to work at this time, instead the time was to be dedicated to beginning to write this book. I still had a reasonable amount of savings, so I heeded his voice and began writing.

Yet as my saved funds depleted quickly, I began to fear and quietly returned to the job search. God reminded me of what he had said to me before, but this time I wasn't really listening. I was too busy paying attention to the voices of fear, and common sense, and the expectations of others. Yes, it is good to work. Yes, we absolutely should earn a living and not expect to receive the charity of others. But one voice speaks above all those things: God's. And in *that* season, and that season only, God directed me towards writing, rather than seeking work elsewhere.

Sadly, in a moment of weakness, I applied for a part-time cleaning job (knowing in my spirit I was being disobedient) and began that job less than a week later. It was a good job and perfect for my level of understanding of the German language at the time; the boss was nice, the work was simple, I was left to get on with it myself, and could listen to worship music and pray as I cleaned. But as my job began, my writing stopped. I radically reduced my available writing time by accepting that job. True, I now had some income, but what I had been called to do in that season was being neglected. I had made the wrong choice. I had listened to the voice of fear. I had pushed past God, through a door which I had no business to open: a door that God had repeatedly told me not to walk through.

I worked that job for just six weeks before an insurance issue forced me to take a break. At first, I was frustrated at the misunderstanding and worked hard to try to resolve it. But as I faced hurdle after hurdle after hurdle, I began to realize that I had walked that wrong path for long enough and God was graciously steering me back through the right door.

I eventually repented of my pride, having thought that I knew what was best, and decided to rejoin God on his path, rather than continuing to seek to carve out my own. I recalled the last instruction God had given me—to write—and decided to obey, even though it made no sense to me.

Within the first week of returning to writing, I received the equivalent of two months' wages from a collection of sources. God, in his grace, showed me that, when we walk in obedience to him, he blesses us far beyond what the world could ever provide.

At 2016's Willow Creek Global Leadership Summit, Jossy Chacko said, "Don't let earthly practicalities cause you to lose sight of the heavenly possibilities." In those weeks, I had. I allowed depleting finances and cultural expectations to shout louder than the voice of the all-sufficient Saviour. And I forfeited witnessing miracles because of my disobedience.

Incredibly, God caused my boss to show me favour and allowed me to keep that job, despite an extended delay in procuring the necessary insurance documents. But there was purpose in the delay. That delay allowed me to finish the first draft of this book. The timing of my return to work fitted perfectly around everything else that God wished me to use those three months for. Finances were tight, but God always made a way, and he provided in other ways that are far more valuable than money. The absence of work hours also made way for opportunities to serve in church and the development of new relationships.

There are open doors, closed doors, and sometimes there are doors that are left ajar, to see how we will respond to God's direction. I failed that test but learnt a valuable lesson. And once again I was reminded that God's promises do not depend on our pathetic strength, but on the faithfulness of the Sovereign Lord.

Around that same time, I began adding a request to my daily prayers: "God, surprise me". And he did! But, to be honest, I'm not even sure he was doing anything different to what he had always done. I believe, by praying these words, my *perspective* changed and my *expectation* increased. Now I anticipate his surprises daily: moments that he orchestrates in my normal routine which reveal his hand at work in the detail of my life. These moments vary from personal encouragements to confirmation of his leading, to participation in conversations that uplift and inspire.

When we live every single day of our lives in constant anticipation of what God could do, how he could act, what doors of opportunity he could open and the miracles he could outwork in the very detail of our lives, we soon learn that God *is* interested in the small things. He cares about the things that we care about, because he loves us. He wants to enter into every decision and action of our day-to-day existence to reveal to us his care, his love and his power.

When we delight ourselves in the Lord—who he is and all that he has done for us—we become more familiar with his heart and, as we grow closer to him, gradually the desires of our hearts align with his. When we commit our ways, our hopes, our future plans to the Lord, we can trust him with everything. And he *will* act on our behalf (Psalm 37:4–5).

The biblical character David is one of the most well-known figures in God's story. He is often best known for his supernatural victory over the giant, Goliath (1 Samuel 17). David later became king of Israel, but his journey from giant-slaying shepherd boy to crowned hero was far from straightforward.

The Lord's prophet, Samuel (whom we read about in chapter 2), had anointed David as God's chosen one to rule his beloved nation when David was just a teenager. Following his defeat over the Philistines, David's fame and popularity as a great warrior grew in Israel. But King Saul became jealous and his love for David quickly turned to hate. So much so, that David had to flee from the palace, where he had personally serenaded King Saul with his harp, and run for his life.

The future looked bleak for David as Saul hunted him. For years he was viciously pursued, yet he was never found. And when David became discouraged and disheartened, his best friend (and Saul's son), Jonathan, was there to remind him of the promises of God: that he, David, would be king over Israel one day.

You see, God had promised that he would take David to the "other side" of this chase, but he needed his faithful friends by his side to encourage him and remind him of that. Aren't godly friends so precious? We cannot and should not walk this life alone. Adventure is far more fun with friends, is it not?

God may have allowed David to be *hunted* by Saul, but God never allowed him to be *found*. In his affliction, God's promise brought David comfort and gave him life (Psalm 119:50).

While the circumstances that David found himself in seemed dire, the tale, from God's perspective, was outworking just as it should. David was living his adventure. A scary one at times, granted, but no adventure is without risk. His adventure was one that would prepare him to be king. It was a journey that tested and built his faith. An experience that revealed to him who his true friends were and illustrated the faithfulness of his God. Though he stared death straight in the face on a number of occasions, David chose to believe what God had said over what he saw around him. "If God is for us, who can be against us?" (Romans 8:31).

But there's a twist to this story. You see, David had the opportunity to take Saul's life, not once but twice. Twice, he had the chance to kill Saul and end this exhausting pursuit. Twice, he could have ended Saul's reign and seized the crown himself, knowing it was to be his soon anyway. But he did not.

David was chosen by God and crowned as king over Israel because he was a man after God's own heart. David possessed the heart of God. Let's just take a moment for that to sink in. Should we not all strive to possess the heart of God? Gosh, I want that.

And because David carried the heart of God, he understood that to take a man's life was a sin. He knew that removing the crown of God's chosen leader in that season was outside the will of his Father. It may have made his circumstances far more comfortable, but David did not wish to choose the *easy* way; he sought to live the *right* way. While his soldiers encouraged him to end Saul there and then, David trusted that God would outwork things his way, without David interfering. The crown would still be his, there was no doubt about that, but he was not going to deceive or manipulate the situation in order to get it.

We can learn a lot from David's actions here. While we anticipate adventure and the fulfilment of God's promises in our lives, we must be careful not to anticipate God's movements or seek to "help" him to outwork his will. Instead, we wait, seek him and what he wishes to say to us, and give him room to act in his own way and timing. We must resist getting in the way, therefore hindering God's plans and being disobedient in the process.

David had to kill Goliath, put up with Saul's jealousy and eventually his rage, counteract Saul's scheming and continue to do his job as an army commander. But the reason he was able to do all these things (and more) was because he knew and understood that God was on his side.

Do you believe that God can and will do what he has said he will do? Are you claiming his promises in your own life? Are you entering into the adventure he has prepared for you?

It is not necessary to have a long-term plan. Plans change, but God remains constant. Proverbs 16:9 reminds us that "The heart of man plans his way, but the Lord establishes his steps." So just commit everything to him and enjoy the present: take it all in. Embrace what is happening *now*. Don't dream away the weeks, the months, the years. Resist placing timelines and expectations on God's promises or, indeed, your own desires. Simply enjoy the now. There are so many experiences in life to be enjoyed and savoured. Live life; stop fixating on what you don't have, and start appreciating what you *do* have.

There is no need to try so hard to fill in the blanks of what God *might* be saying or doing in your life. He will give you the information you need when you need it; you have no reason to strive. Instead of stressing about what those "meanwhile" moments look like, just enjoy them and rest in God's ways and timing. Don't take on the burden yourself. God's will is not a problem to solve; it is a gift to receive at the appointed time:

> For still the vision awaits its appointed time; it hastens to the end—it will not lie. If it seems slow, wait for it; it will surely come; it will not delay.
>
> *Habakkuk 2:3*

9
Packing Light

Heading home from New York City after my internship, I knew that my suitcase was overweight. I had tried to get rid of as much as I could before I left, but, after three months abroad, I not only carried my belongings home with me, but many sentimental items too. There were gifts from the teenagers I had worked with, hand-drawn cards from some of the kids, not to mention my team T-shirts, a scrapbook and two leadership binders I had accumulated during my training.

At the airport, I gingerly approached the check-in desk, laden down with a full-to-bursting suitcase and a backpack stuffed with all my heavy items. I swung my case onto the conveyor belt and watched the numbers on the scale shoot upwards.

"I'm sorry," said the airline attendant, "your case is too heavy. You will need to remove something."

"Can't I just pay the overweight fee?" I asked, wondering how on earth I could possibly fit anything more into my backpack.

"You don't understand," she replied politely, but with a slight bite in her words. "Your case exceeds the overweight limit. You must remove something in addition to paying the overweight fee."

Eugh. It was the last thing I needed when I was tired and anxious to get home to my family for Christmas after my extended absence. I hauled the suitcase back off the conveyor belt and slid it to the side, so as not to get in the way of other passengers. I did not relish the idea of all my belongings being on show for passers-by, but there was no way around it; I had to lighten the load.

My hands dived into the carefully packed trunk, feeling around for something I dared to part with. I tried to pick the smaller, but heavier items and cram them into my backpack. I also had a handbag and a mono-strapped camera bag that I was able to drape over me to relieve some of the pressure on my suitcase. Hoping I had done enough, I dragged it back across to the woman at the desk for another weigh-in.

Fortunately, my extra effort had had the required effect, and my suitcase was now accepted for check-in. I stumbled away from the desk wearing all my heavy items but with my purse noticeably lighter.

It had not been the first time I had been charged for overweight baggage, and it certainly would not be the last. But the fact of the matter was, I could not travel to my next destination without emptying my case a little. And this is true for us spiritually, too.

We all carry baggage: hurt, anger, resentment, pride, shame, fear, mistrust, bitterness, withheld forgiveness. They are all things we have picked up along the way through our journey called life. But in order for us to move forward into new seasons, we need to leave some of these items behind. If we insist on bringing our extra baggage with us, we can count on there being a hefty price to pay further down the line.

When I was faced with the issue of extra baggage in NYC, all I did was move the problem from one bearer (my suitcase) to another (myself)! That may have satisfied the airline regulations, but it did not really solve the problem; I still carried the same excess weight onto the plane. But with our own issues and hang-ups, moving them from one place to another, suppressing the hurt and anger deep down, or simply ignoring the problem altogether, will do nothing to lighten the load. Those issues will continue to fester like mould in our hearts until they are dealt with properly.

Fortunately, we have our very own, and very willing, baggage handler: God. He knows what we have packed away into the corners and crevices of our hearts, better than we often know ourselves. He also relishes the opportunity to help us to clear some space—God is no hoarder!

He has had to handle a whole truck full of my luggage on my adventure so far. Each new season has begun by facing some of the hidden items, which over time had become intrinsic to my being, and off-loading a few of these to make my journey that little bit easier. The deeper we dug together, the more surprised I was to find that I had been holding onto scars and false ideas that had formed decades ago. It is great to be rid of so many old and tired containers and feel the heaviness lifted. The off-loading itself, however, can be painful.

In order for us to be most effective in our pursuit of God's best for us, we must be vulnerable and humble before him. There is nothing that we can expose to God that he does not already know, but the very act of confession and surrender before God begins a healing work in our hearts and gives him permission to begin gently extracting the battered, old suitcases that we have long hidden away.

The good news is this: as he begins to remove the extra baggage, one item at a time, it creates more space for him to fill with other things—good things!—such as his love, his acceptance, his power, and his dreams for your future.

Our biggest item of baggage that we all begin life with is sin. But when we commit to living our lives for God and ask him for his forgiveness, he lifts that burden off our backs and hangs it on the cross with Jesus. Yet the effects and consequences of sin often linger.

We all battle sin. Every single one of us has an internal predisposition to sin because of Adam and Eve's original sin in the Garden of Eden. But our attitude towards sin *is* something that we can control. God detests sin, so the more we invite him to play an active role in our lives, the more we will become like him, and the more we, too, will hate sin. Our attitude towards sin will change as we grow to be more like Christ, resulting in a diminished desire to *want* to sin. Through Jesus' saving work on the cross, we can all claim freedom from sin and, thank God, he looks on those of us who have accepted his salvation as right and sinless in his eyes. We can claim Christ's victory over sin for ourselves.

However, living in this victory does not come without a fight. The fight against sin is one that we will enter into daily until the day we die, or until Jesus returns to take those who love him to be with him for eternity. It is a fight that is impossible to win in our own strength, but the more we depend on God and draw close to him, the easier the fight will become. By allowing God to remove those bags of sinful habits—lying, greed, gossiping, envy, selfishness and so many others—deeply rooted in our hearts, we create more space for him to reside there, and he not only equips us to fight the sinful desires that remain, but his presence repels that which we once found appealing.

Jesus told a parable in Luke 15 about a man with two sons. The younger son came to his father one day and asked, somewhat cheekily, for his half of the family's inheritance. What he was really saying to his very-much-alive father was: "You are not important to me; you are as good as dead. All I am interested in is your money." But the father graciously offered his younger son the inheritance due to him.

Having received his half of the family's wealth, the son packed up his belongings and left home. He travelled around, squandering his inheritance and partying hard. But, inevitably, his funds eventually ran out. A famine hit the land and he found himself in desperate need.

In his search for work, he found a man who hired him to feed the pigs on his farm. As he stared longingly at the food the pigs were eating, he thought to himself: "My father's servants get fed better than this, and here I am starving! I'll return to my father and ask to be a servant in his home, because I am no longer worthy to be treated as a son."

He got up and began the long, lonely walk back to his father's house. But while he was still far from the house, his father spotted him and was filled with compassion. He ran to meet his son and embraced him tightly. "Father," implored the son, perhaps ashamed to even look his father in the eye, "I am no longer worthy to be called your son." But his father threw his best robe over his son's shoulders, placed a ring on his son's finger and new shoes on his feet.

"Tonight, we celebrate!" exclaimed the father, "for my son has returned. He was dead, but is alive again. He was lost, but has been found."

Jesus painted this picture so that we could glimpse the love of our Heavenly Father. We act foolishly, or use God for our own selfish ambition, but when we return to him, he welcomes us with open arms! There is no judgement or price to be paid, for Jesus has already done that for us. Instead, the Father celebrates that we have returned home to him.

A few years back, I hit a really low point. It may not have been particularly obvious to those around me because outwardly everything went on as normal; I continued working in full-time ministry, I continued serving in church and I continued attending worship services. But my internal world was a mess. You see, I had allowed a pattern of sin to develop in my life and the guilt and shame that came with it was nearly too much to handle.

For as long as I could remember, I desired to be married and have a family. But as I careered towards thirty—still single, with no potential husband in sight—my mind became a battle-zone. Though I was not living in the reality of my dream, I began to live it in my mind. Glamourized Hollywood love scenes would play through my thoughts, and my purity was compromised. I did not need images to stimulate me, because my imagination was vivid enough.

I began to believe the lie that this—all that the media portrays—was what real love looked like. And that is what I craved. Yet, deep down inside, I knew this was not what God wanted for me.

Knowing my imagination needed curbing, I began to take measures to reduce the stimulation. I stopped watching movies or TV series that were rated above "suitable for twelve years and over". I got rid of the DVDs that I owned that had vivid love scenes or nudity. I took simple measures to help protect myself from the sin that threatened to burst into addiction. I tried everything I could to change my habits but that was not enough. Only Jesus could kill this sin once and for all.

Accepting God's forgiveness, as incredible as it is, is not usually something I struggle with. Learning to forgive myself, on the other hand, has proved far more challenging. It was this very problem that led to guilt, shame and condemnation. But if God forgives us, then is it not an insult to Jesus' work on the cross to withhold forgiveness from ourselves?

The weight I carried was sucking the life out of me. For every time I slipped up, the burden I carried would grow. Soon, the sin was no longer the main issue, but the guilt and shame that it resulted in. The spiritual fire that had once burned so brightly in me was reduced to a glowing ember and I distanced myself from God and from others. But that was a mistake.

I truly thought that I had entirely ruined my chances of ever being useful to God again. All those dreams that I had once carried and the purposes he had called me to seemed to sink into the abyss of my shame.

The truth was, God had never left me. In fact, as I reflect on that dark period, it is incredible to recognize the prayers he answered and the way he guided me, even when I was too ashamed to seek him. I can see now that he had already begun working on some of the underlying issues that pained my fragile heart, those scars that had led me to this point. He did not condemn me. He did not heap shame on me. He *loved* me.

And he was the only one who could pull me out of the pit that I had dug for myself.

I had never wanted to be in this mess. I had consistently asked God for his help and his power to overcome the lust in my heart. But it wasn't until I began to understand the root of the problem—the insecurities and lies that had pushed me into these sinful habits in the first place—that I was able to begin to allow God to chip away at the sin itself.

My focus had always remained on the problem, and that was my mistake. If I tell you not to think about elephants, what immediately pops into your head? Elephants, right? I had been living with one eye on God and one eye on my sin. But until I fixed both eyes on him, the problem remained.

When we want to break bad habits and deal with the sin in our lives, we must humble ourselves and call out to God to deal with it for us. Sometimes that is the last thing we feel like doing, because the guilt and shame we carry is too much. But God is a loving God who convicts us and seeks to help us overcome. He does not shame us or condemn us; instead he watches the horizon, waiting for our return, and runs out to meet us with open arms.

Gently, step by step, God began to restore what was broken in my life. He gave me a new understanding of true love. He removed the guilt and shame that had weighed so heavily on me. He corrected the lies of insecurity and worthlessness that I had been carrying for so long. Like the father of the Prodigal Son, God threw his loving arms around me and celebrated that I had returned to him, not in a perfect, polished state, but broken and dirty, in need of his embrace.

The future that I had once hoped for but thought I had lost, was slowly and graciously restored. My Heavenly Father accepted me and repeatedly spoke words of affirmation and love over me in the months that followed. I feared that my mistakes had cost me my dreams but, in fact, they were the making of me. What the enemy meant for harm, God used for good. His love, his pursuit of me, his grace and forgiveness were more real to me than ever before. I learnt what real love is, and I learnt to love myself. I began to see myself how God sees me, and I felt safe in his acceptance of me. Psalm 34:22 declares a comforting truth: "The Lord redeems the life of his servants; none of those who take refuge in him will be condemned."

When I finally turned my full attention to Jesus, the rest of my problems began to melt away. And this is true in whatever difficulties we are facing; when we keep Jesus at the centre of every aspect of our lives, the issues don't seem so overwhelming. Our priority is to draw close to him, and he will, in his goodness, take care of everything else.

The more I grow in love with Jesus, the more disappointed I am with myself when I do sin. But the enemy no longer has the opportunity to use one slip-up to drag me back down into the depths of despair, because now I have a far greater understanding and appreciation of God's great grace, mercy, love and forgiveness. I am *so* grateful. I am not worthy, yet he chose me, loved me, sent his Son to die for me, and he looks at me and smiles because of what Christ did for me. That's something incredible.

The enemy is still out to bring you, and me, down. He does not want you to thrive in your adventure so he will do everything in his power to disable you. He will remind you of the baggage you still carry. He will echo the lies you believe about yourself. He will encourage you to compare yourself to others around you, urging you to conclude that you fall short, that you are of no use to God, that you have wandered too far to ever receive grace and forgiveness.

But this is absolutely not true:

> With the arrival of Jesus, the Messiah, that fateful dilemma is resolved. Those who enter into Christ's being-here-for-us no longer have to live under a continuous, low-lying black cloud. A new power is in operation. The Spirit of life in Christ, like a strong wind, has magnificently cleared the air, freeing you from a fated lifetime of brutal tyranny at the hands of sin and death. God went for the jugular when he sent his own Son. He didn't deal with the problem as something remote and unimportant. In his Son, Jesus, he personally took on the human condition, entered the disordered mess of struggling humanity in order to set it right once and for all. The law code, weakened as it always was by fractured human nature, could never have done that. The law always ended up being used as a Band-Aid on sin instead of a deep healing of it. And now what the law code asked for but we couldn't deliver is accomplished as we, instead of redoubling

our own efforts, simply embrace what the Spirit is doing in us. Those who think they can do it on their own end up obsessed with measuring their own moral muscle but never get around to exercising it in real life. Those who trust God's action in them find that God's Spirit is in them—living and breathing God! Obsession with self in these matters is a dead end; attention to God leads us out into the open, into a spacious, free life.

Romans 8:1-6, The Message

That is the beauty of God's love. Love overcomes imperfections and flaws, weaknesses and sin.

When we take steps into our adventure, we can count on the enemy's attack. Any advance we make towards identifying and dismissing the lies we believe is a danger to his strategy. When we deal with insecurities, and hurts from our past, he panics, because his offensive has been weakened. Choosing to forgive those who have wronged you will make him mad. You can bet he will look for other ways to distract you and sway you back off course. But remember this: the enemy may be big, but God is bigger. We need to establish ourselves firmly in the Word of God to resist the enemy and his efforts.

It is not easy to share our deepest struggles or insecurities, but sharing them in a safe place with trusted individuals brings freedom and breaks the hold of sin in your life. The enemy loves to work in secret, filling your mind with lies and doubts that drive you away from God and from others. But community interrupts those destructive patterns and allows the voice of truth to break in. Find someone who you can open up to: someone who is discreet, who can be trusted, and is seeking to live a godly life; someone who cares more about your faith than your comfort. Talk to them about how you are feeling and ask them to journey with you and to hold you accountable. The great thing about having someone who walks alongside you through the struggle is that they are also there to celebrate with you when you experience breakthrough!

We often want to get all the kinks of our lives worked out before we answer God's call to adventure, but that is not how he works. God calls those who feel that they have nothing to offer to do his greatest work. He chooses those who know they need his help over those who think they can do it themselves. The very things that you have allowed to rot for so long—those putrid items in the hold of your heart—are the tools he wants to use to set others free. He uses the adventure to purify your life. Your testimony will pave the way for someone else's freedom.

Remember, God wastes nothing. The battles we conquer and the lessons we learn become powerful weapons in our arsenal to lead others out of the darkness and into God's glorious light.

In the previous chapter, we learnt a little about David, a man after God's own heart. So would it surprise you, then, to learn that he messed up too? Big time. His lustful thoughts led him into adultery and fathering an illegitimate child, which eventually led him to commit murder in an attempt to hide his failings. But that did not end his work for the Lord. David had to pay the price for his sin, but he repented and God restored their relationship. Despite his mistakes, David left a godly legacy and the Son of God, Jesus Christ, was born through his bloodline.

In my twenties, I realized that I was carrying a hefty suitcase around, labelled "coping mechanisms". I whipped it out regularly and rummaged through it to find a strategy or mindset that I could adopt that might help me respond to the circumstances I faced. I even employed my bag of tricks in my walk with God. I failed to recognize that God had good things prepared for me, and that he was working all things together for my good (Romans 8:28). Instead, in every situation I faced, I was expecting the worst to save myself from disappointment, but all that says to God is, "I don't trust you to look after my heart."

Many of my thoughts and actions at that time were fuelled by guilt. I wasn't necessarily afraid of the destiny God had for me, but I was afraid of the opinions of others, of making wrong decisions and of disappointing people as I transitioned into new seasons. But if God had called me into something new, he would not neglect me during those "middle" moments.

Around this same time, I was also really struggling to accept God's unconditional love. I was either working too hard to try to earn it, or I was rejecting it because I didn't think that I deserved it. I constantly needed to remind myself (and choose to *accept*) that God loves me, he created me, he has a great plan for me, he died for me, he saved me, he chose me, and he won't let go, no matter what I have done or will do in the future. This truth, once realized, entirely transformed my relationship with God, and my relationships with others too, because I learnt to accept love without conditions, and this brought freedom and security.

When we refuse to deal with our extra baggage, we tend to default to Spiritual Autopilot. This is such a dangerous thing. We work, and we serve, and we minister, and we give until we are running on fumes, but unless we take the time to refuel at the feet of the Father, our efforts will be fruitless. Besides, if we are so crammed full of unnecessary baggage, there will be little room for the fuel of the Holy Spirit to work within us anyway! When we stifle the work of the Holy Spirit, our efforts become wearisome because we become dependent only on our own strength, and not the infinite resources of God.

While operating on Spiritual Autopilot, there is no growth, no progress and no room for *response*. If we want to keep moving forward into the best that God has for us, then we must be continually tuned into his voice to know which way to turn. Depending on a pre-set programme is not an option. In order to maintain a healthy, growing relationship with God, we must be intentional, responsive and obedient. Just as with any healthy human relationship, open and honest communication is key. So be careful not to let extra baggage get in the way of that.

Sometimes God suggests an item of baggage that needs to be off-loaded; other times he waits for us to lay it before him. He's not going to force us to deal with it, but he knows we can't deal with it alone. It needs to be dealt with, and he is the best person for the job. He loves to roll up his sleeves and get to work on that full-to-bursting trunk stuffed into the corner of your heart.

What can you begin dealing with today? What pain or hurt are you carrying that God would gladly take off your hands? Has something already popped into your mind? If so, give it over to him; he will be gentle. Confess to him the problem and your helplessness in that situation and he will begin to do a healing work in your heart. If you are not sure what to deal with first, ask God where he wants to begin. Pray about it, and I guarantee you will soon identify something out of place in your heart that needs to be left behind. Just pick an item of hand-luggage and start with that.

It took many months for me to finally leave the lustful thoughts behind. Months of praying, of returning to God and repenting when I slipped up, of allowing God to rewire my heart into a greater understanding of the love he has for us and the love he calls each of us to. But, one by one, he removed the bags crammed full of condemnation, guilt, shame, and the deep-rooted issues that had led to this sin in the first place. I have no room to carry those extra bags anymore, because I am running the race that God has mapped out for me and navigating this wonderful, faith-filled adventure with him.

1 0

When Adventure Becomes a Habit

I was never much of an adventurer growing up. I was the kid who watched as her friends hurtled around on a rollercoaster while I stood safely on solid ground. As a teenager, I held my peers' belongings as they climbed and swung and scrambled their way through the ropes course at summer camp. Even in my early years of adulthood, every venture was perfectly planned and the risks conscientiously calculated. To me, spontaneity was a bad word.

My sanity revolved around well-constructed plans determined to the smallest detail, with every possible outcome weighed and accounted for. Any waver in those plans and fear descended upon me as my mind worked frantically to assess and avoid potential problems. Because of these habits, I used to think that being so organized and reasoned in my thinking was a poor character trait. But what I've since realized is that it is not the skill itself (indeed, a God-given gift) that is the problem, but the attitude and premise behind it.

My motive for considering every detail had always been control, whether I had realized it at the time or not. I liked to be prepared so, naturally, I felt the need to examine every possible outcome so that I could prepare for it. Any deviation in my plan, however, would render me stressed and anxious. That anxiety would manifest itself in a variety of ways: trouble sleeping, repeatedly playing out various scenarios over and over in my head, rehearsing conversations if I anticipated conflict and confrontation, tension in relationships . . . essentially, I just drove myself crazy!

The reality was, of course, that I was never in control to begin with. By desiring to control, I had actually placed myself in God's role (no wonder

I experienced so much anxiety!). At the root of this need to control I was simply stating that "my ways are better than God's ways". Ouch.

Fast-forward a number of years and many valuable lessons later, I have let go of my need to control because I recognize and personally know the One who is truly sovereign over all things. I know he loves me more than I could ever imagine, and therefore his plans for me are good and will not lead to disaster. That does not mean I am promised an easy life, but I have broadened my perspective to see that my life is about more than just me and my own comfort.

My life is to be lived in worship of the Almighty God who created me, saved me, redeemed me and has purposed me for greater things. My life is an instrument in God's hands to be used for the growth of his kingdom, so that others may experience the love, forgiveness and freedom that I know. My life is a dynamic, visible expression of God's power and glory. My life is not about me. But here's the best part: when we surrender our lives and prioritize God's purposes over our own, he will shower us with gifts, abundant provision, daily surprises and opportunities far out of our own reach. He will give us the life that we didn't know we wanted, one far beyond what we could dream up or achieve for ourselves. This is what life looks like when adventure becomes a habit.

I no longer need to feel extensively prepared for the situations I face—whether forecasted or not—because I trust God to meet every need in *every* outcome. I still have to be a good steward of what he gives me, but the best way to prepare for any outcome, I realized, is to consistently and entirely depend on God. When I relinquish control, I create opportunity for my faith to grow.

My perspective has been completely transformed since my formative years, and his peace is what now guides me. In relinquishing control I've experienced a new freedom; my once mundane and highly regimented daily routine is now viewed through the eyes of an Indiana-Jones-like adventurer, anticipating all the surprises God has in store for me every single day! I am still organized—yes. I still make plans—of course. *But I hold them loosely in my hands.* I am no longer seeking to control the outcomes of these plans like I once did, because I rest assured in God's sovereign purposes for my life and know that, no matter what I face, *he* is the answer that I need.

If everything in our life was certain, I reckon we would either be epically bored or incredibly afraid. Can you imagine knowing what was to come, knowing what you would face in a few weeks, months, years? Would that really bring you peace? I don't think so. What about in relationships? Would we want to definitively know every opinion, every thought of our friend or spouse? Surely not. There can be no trust, no relationship, if there is no freedom.

American author John Ortberg wrote: "We all think we want certainty. But we don't. What we really want is trust, wisely placed. Trust is better than certainty because it honours the freedom of persons and makes possible growth and intimacy that certainty alone could never produce."[18]

The same is true in our relationship with God. When there is certainty in our circumstances, faith becomes obsolete. Faith is no longer faith when the outcome is certain, but faith in a certain God, who holds an infinite number of possibilities in the palm of his hand, is a faith that thrives. Faith surrenders everything to God and anticipates a good outcome. Faith remains steadfast even in the midst of doubts and unanswered questions. Faith relinquishes control and permits God to solve our problems for us; we rarely understand *how* God will act, but we remain sure that he *will*.

We need to stop viewing uncertainty as such a terrible thing. Indeed, it is not upon certainty that we seek to place our trust, but upon the feeble plans that we have made ourselves (as if our plans are ever certain!) and in which we try to find some comfort. But when our peace is dependent on circumstances, it is not real peace. Let's be honest, our comfort zones are not really all that comfortable. We spend so much time and energy trying to maintain the delicate balance of status quo that we rarely have the opportunity to actually make ourselves comfortable. Rather, true peace is dependent on our trust in God, regardless of our circumstances. The only thing we can be certain of is anything that is spoken forth by the voice of God; his Word alone is certain.

Believe it or not, there is fun and adventure to be found in uncertainty! When our faith is firmly rooted in God, we welcome the surprises that uncertainty brings because we are assured that God has a purpose; he can bring good from any situation. We have to trust his plan, trust his timing and trust that he loves us and is motivated by that love. Uncertainty paves the way for miracles and God-ordained "coincidences". We can either choose to face uncertainty worrying about all that could go wrong, or face it with anticipation of all that God will bring about through it. Nothing is uncertain to him.

Growing up, I remember my uncle telling me: "Faith is spelled R. I. S. K." But there is a clear difference between a foolish risk and an inspired risk. A risk motivated by rebellion, irresponsibility or selfish gain is one that will likely cost far more than we anticipate, whether we pay for it now or much later. But a risk taken by faith and in obedience to God is an action that declares to the world, "If God doesn't come through for me, I'm in big trouble!"

An inspired risk is one that lays all our hope on the One that has called us. It is a response to God that depends entirely on his faithfulness and provision, for it would be impossible in our own strength. When our circumstances scream at us to run in the opposite direction, faith encourages us to charge ahead. The conviction in our hearts is what strengthens us to keep going. That is an inspired risk. That is faith.

And with the Almighty God on our side, we should be the biggest risk-takers on earth. When the shepherd boy David faced Goliath, he did not hesitate in stepping forward, because he understood that he was not facing the giant alone:

> You come to me with a sword and with a spear and with a javelin, but I come to you in the name of the Lord of hosts, the God of the armies of Israel, whom you have defied. This day the Lord will deliver you into my hand, and I will strike you down and cut off your head. And I will give the dead bodies of the host of the Philistines this day to the birds of the air and to the wild beasts of the earth, that all the earth may know that there is a God in Israel, and that all this assembly may know that the Lord saves not with sword and spear. For the battle is the Lord's, and he will give you into our hand.
>
> *1 Samuel 17:45–7*

That is not the war cry of a man who is uncertain! He knows his God and has the faith to take a risk to save his people from total devastation. David placed himself in an entirely vulnerable situation, knowing that he would die if God did not come through for him, yet he did not waver. David did not question whether he should put his life on the line, because he believed that God would show up. He believed that the God who had rescued him from lions and bears as he watched over his sheep, would protect him once again on this day as he faced a greater challenge than ever before. He trusted that the God who had anointed him as the next king of Israel would fulfil his promise and not allow him to perish before his time. That is faith.

2 Corinthians 9:6 promises: "Whoever sows sparingly will also reap sparingly, and whoever sows bountifully will also reap bountifully." This is true of our finances, our love, our gifts and talents, but I believe it is also true of our faith. When we operate in little faith, we see very little of God's power. But when we throw all common sense and control out the window in pursuit of God, he will show us his power in unimaginable ways. Don't you want to develop the kind of faith that confronts giants, defeats armies with a shout of victory, or walks on water? Then we need to exercise it.

During one of my trips to New York City I had no agenda; I simply allowed God to lead me around the city. I walked, I prayed, I stopped and had coffee, I read a book. And all the while I watched for opportunities for the Holy Spirit to prompt me into action.

Having become lost in Greenwich Village, I met a homeless man named Malik. Our interaction was brief, but I took him to the nearest store and bought him lunch while exchanging some chit-chat. He remarked that I must be from out of town because New Yorkers never stopped or paid any attention to him.

The next day, as I sat on a bench in Central Park reading my book, I was nervously approached by two Christian college girls who asked if they could pray for me. It was their first day in the city as part of a short-term mission team, so I graciously returned the favour and encouraged them as they embarked on their outreach in the Big Apple.

As I returned home on the subway that evening, I spotted a woman who was struggling to juggle all her shopping as well as her young family. I simply offered to carry her pushchair up the stairs to ground level.

None of these acts are particularly noteworthy, but they were small acts that made a big difference to those individuals in their moment of need.

As I walked around the city, I saw so many people facing challenges and desperately in need of Jesus—homelessness, aggressive or rude attitudes, people struggling with their identity or sexuality, idolatry of material possessions—the list goes on. But there are people with those same needs in every town and city around the world. We can all do something; we just need to be alert to opportunity.

Perhaps you are waiting for the right ministry role, the right spouse, the right job, believing that those things will bring with them adventure. But adventure is less about your circumstances and more about your attitude towards them.

We cannot live our lives always waiting for the next "big thing". Spending our time focusing on the big thing that we want (even if it is a God-given desire) causes us to miss out on every little thing occurring along the way. Learning to be content with the present—whatever that may look like—is learning to trust that God knows what he is doing. He knows what good gifts to give you and when to give them. If there is discontentment in your heart, then identify why that is and ask God to help meet that need. Use your frustrations and passions to drive your holy pursuit after God. Don't miss out on today's adventure because you are too busy dreaming about tomorrow's.

Living a life of faith and adventure is not just about the big milestones either. We need God *daily*. We need to invite him to be part of our everyday, run-of-the-mill, just-another-day-at-the-office kind of days. This journey is not to be embarked upon alone; he promises to walk with us. We don't just need him for the big steps; we need him for every step in between too.

In the book of Exodus we read about a man named Moses (we touched briefly on his life and the plight of the Israelites in a previous chapter). Moses was born in Egypt to an Israelite, but Pharaoh, king of Egypt, was afraid that the Israelites were growing too numerous and feared they would rise up against him. Therefore, Pharaoh put the Israelites to work as his slaves, to weaken them and remind them who was boss. He also commanded that all baby boys born to Israelite families should be killed to purge the nation of Israel, and Moses was one such baby.

But God had a special purpose for Moses' life. Moses' mother tucked him up in a basket and hid him among the reeds on the River Nile in an effort to spare his life. As his sister watched, Moses was found by Pharaoh's daughter, and she took him to the palace and raised him there as her own son.

When he was grown, Moses watched in horror, one day, as an Egyptian beat one of his own people, an Israelite. Enraged, he killed the Egyptian and hid him in the sand. But Moses grew afraid when he realized that his deed was known to Pharaoh, who sought retribution for the murder of one of his men, so Moses fled into the desert. There he remained for forty years.

In those forty years Moses tended sheep, married the daughter of a Midianite priest and started a family with her. For decades Moses lived in relative obscurity, no doubt choosing to forget the events of his past and settling comfortably into his new, much humbler abode. I reckon that he expected to remain there for the rest of his days, with no plans of his own to return to the land of his birth. But God was just getting started . . .

Though Moses hadn't known it, God had been carefully and purposefully steering him through life, until God's appointed time to reveal himself. Four decades were what was needed to prepare Moses for his God-ordained adventure, and then God began to unveil his plan.

Moses still had to overcome fear in order to carry out all that God had called him to do, but he trusted God and was obedient to him. He was not perfect—he made mistakes like the rest of us—but as Moses grew in faith and obedience, God's power grew within him. During his time in the wilderness, Moses encountered God, was instructed by God and was equipped by God. Then God told him, "Go!"

I love to read about Moses. He is one of my favourite biblical characters, because he is just an ordinary man who was called by God into an extraordinary destiny. Every step of obedience led to greater opportunity, greater responsibility and greater miracles. He is one of the few men or women in the Bible that we have the privilege of tracking throughout their entire life, and not just seeing a window into their lives for a short period of time. This allows us to follow Moses' entire adventure, from start to finish, for all the big moments and every season in between.

Just like us, Moses had to first encounter God and learn about his Creator. Depending on the tales of his Israelite heritage was not enough to prepare him for the great tasks God would call him to. Moses had to discover the great I AM for himself. He needed to know God personally.

Next, Moses journeyed to discover who *he* was and the special purpose God had in mind for him. It was no coincidence, after all, that Moses had been found by none other than royalty when he had been hidden from Pharaoh's men as a baby. Though he had been brought up in the Egyptian palace, he was an Israelite and deeply cared for his own people. And as God shared with Moses all that he was calling him to do, he helped Moses to overcome his insecurities and the doubts that filled his mind.

God then ensured that Moses was well equipped for the adventure he was about to undertake, demonstrating his own power and some of the miracles he would perform. God provided everything that Moses would need, including his own brother, Aaron, to assist him in speaking with Pharaoh.

Moses faced opposition and challenges time and time again, but he always knew exactly where to take them; he repeatedly turned to the Lord for help and guidance. He also waited, sometimes for decades, for God's guidance into the next season. As Moses walked in obedience, God responded faithfully, and, for Moses, adventure with God became a habit. He was in constant anticipation of what God would do next. He did not cringe or cower at seemingly impossible situations because his trust—developed throughout his lifetime—was in an unwavering God.

God used Moses to save the Israelite nation from Egypt and from the hands of Pharaoh, and lead them into the desert. The Israelites would eventually reach the promised land, as vowed to Abraham many years earlier, but that was not to be part of Abraham's or, indeed, Moses' adventure. It would become part of someone else's adventure. Instead, Moses' chapter included confronting an angry king and leading a daring escape from captivity. God was the author of the Israelites' tale, and he authors each of our stories as well; he decides when to feature us as the hero.

Having finally been released from Egypt, Israel began their long trek through the desert on their journey to the promised land. Meanwhile, God caused Pharaoh to change his mind, and he ordered his chariots to pursue the Israelite slaves and return them to Egypt. ("But why?" you might ask. "Why would God *cause* that to happen?" Well, keep reading

. . . God does *nothing* without reason.) As the dust rose from beneath the hooves of the thundering horses, the Israelites panicked. They were faced with the Red Sea ahead of them and Pharaoh's angry horde behind them.

Then Moses turned to the people and announced: "Fear not, stand firm, and see the salvation of the Lord, which he will work for you today. For the Egyptians whom you see today, you shall never see again. The Lord will fight for you, and you have only to be silent" (Exodus 14:13–14).

Moses, as leader of the Israelite people, could have panicked in that moment also. He could have shouldered all the responsibility of saving them from this sticky situation. He could have despaired at their bad luck. But Moses knew better than that. Moses now lived every day as an adventure; he was no longer the timid man he once was. He had learnt that the outcome of this situation was not his responsibility, as long as he walked in faithful obedience to God. He had no answers for the people; instead he pointed them to the One who did.

The *Lord* will fight for you. *He* will work for you. See the salvation of the *Lord*.

"Let's do this together, Moses," was God's response. "You do this, I'll do that, and we'll rescue our people together."

Moses listened and obeyed, God brought his unrivalled power and the people of Israel walked through the parted Red Sea to safety. Why was it so easy for Moses to hear and obey God when he asked him to hold his hand out over the sea? A body of water does not simply part if you wave your hand over it! But Moses had seen God do it before. He had already experienced God's power and seen evidence of God's miraculous ability. And with every step forward, his faith grew, as did his knowledge of the God of Israel.

This miracle was staged by God; it was the perfect set-up to reveal his power. Until that point, few had identified God's hand in the events that had led to the Israelites' departure from Egypt. But now, well *now*, God had everyone's attention! Not only was the entire Israelite nation assembled for this great act of God, but he had prompted Pharaoh to bring his entire army too! No-one present that day missed the hand of God at work.

That day, the Israelite nation turned to God and trusted him and his chosen leader, Moses. That day, the entire Egyptian army perished when

God lifted his hand and the waters of the Red Sea rushed back into place. That day, the Israelites were truly free, their enemy could no longer pursue them and God's power and glory had been displayed for all present.

We may not yet have the faith to hold our hands over the sea and believe that God will part it, but we do have the faith for what God is asking us to do next. Whatever that may be, big or small, muster up the courage and step out in faith. Remind yourself of what he has already done in you and through you. Call to mind the countless times you have seen his faithful answers to prayer or miraculous intervention in your difficulties. Strengthen yourself in the Lord and believe that he will act again, even if your circumstances say otherwise.

A number of years ago I had the opportunity to visit Montenegro as part of a short-term mission team. My local church in Scotland was partnered with a church in the Montenegrin capital city, Podgorica, but our work was primarily with three Balkan refugee camps in the eastern town of Berane. The first team that went out in 2010 were involved in installing a toilet block in the camp which we affectionately called "The Container Camp" because the families there lived in metal shipping containers.

Upon their return, the team gave a presentation to the church about all that they had done on their trip. On that particular night, I happened to be staffing the information desk at the back of the church. And on that particular night, I carried in my hands extra information about our Montenegro partnership, including a sign-up sheet for people interested in participating in the next trip.

As the team shared their experience, they explained the different initiatives they had been involved with in the camp, including work with the children and maintenance work to improve the basic facilities that were available. They told stories of a head lice infestation amongst the young ones and shared photos of team members knee-deep in sewage. Then they called for volunteers to be part of the next team that would visit a few months later.

I don't consider myself to be a particularly "high maintenance" kinda gal, but I do appreciate my home comforts like my hair straighteners. Somehow, I didn't think this was the kind of trip that had time (or need) for hair straighteners, so I was ready to politely decline the team's request. But God had other ideas . . .

Nothing in me *wanted* to join that next team, yet something in me knew I had to. My mind began to race, my heartbeat quickened and everything around me swirled in slow motion. I was terrified to volunteer, but it was an excited, expectant kind of fear. It was like my hand had a mind of its own, and before the team's presentation had even ended, the sign-up sheet lying on the desk in front of me already had my name scribbled at the top.

For the next three years I participated in the annual aid trips to those Montenegrin refugee camps. I fell in love with the people and longed to make more of a difference in their lives. I delighted in building relationships with the individuals, especially the children, in each camp, and endeavoured to learn just a few words of their language so that we could communicate and play games together.

But that third return trip very nearly did not happen. You see, my personal finances were a struggle that year and common sense told me I could not afford to go. I had already agreed to co-lead the team, however, so the question was not *if* I was going, but *how*. I had little more than the amount required for the first instalment, but I was worried about clearing out my bank account, leaving me broke for the remainder of the month. Not to mention my concern over where the rest of the fees would come from when the second instalment was due.

I pondered my predicament over lunch with a friend one day and explained the situation. I did not want to miss out on being part of the trip, but my circumstances had me feeling defeated. Yet we have learnt that God is not defeated by circumstantial evidence. If he wants something to happen, it will happen.

As the deadline for the first payment drew ever closer, I continued to pray and consider the best way to move forward. Somewhat reluctantly, I decided to take a risk. I recall journaling about it and stating, almost in diva-like fashion, that God would just *have* to come through for me. He had put me in this predicament, and therefore he would just have to get me out! So, only a day ahead of the deadline, I cleared out my bank account and paid the first instalment.

And then the miracles began to tally.

The very next day, I received a cheque in the mail from the friend I had previously had lunch with. She had spoken with her husband after we had met, and they had felt compelled to give me a financial gift. The amount matched the first instalment I had paid not twenty-four hours before.

A week or two later, I was approached at the end of the church service by a member of the church finance team. This was nothing particularly unusual, as his work would sometimes overlap with mine, but our conversation that day was not about business.

"Someone would like to give towards your Montenegro trip," he told me. "For the next three months, they will contribute towards the remainder of your fees."

And they did just that. To this day, I have no idea who that anonymous supporter was, but I am incredibly grateful for their generous contribution which provided for me in ways beyond just financial. I couldn't believe it; my entire trip fees had been covered, and God had proved himself faithful once again. But he was not done yet.

Around that same time, I came home one day to find an envelope had been slid under the front door of my apartment. It had clearly been personally delivered, and only had my name scribbled on the front, with no indication of who or where it had come from. And inside was a small sum of cash. The mystery of that gift was never solved either.

Then shortly before we left the country, I received a final financial gift. This gift covered the cost of my spending money and the petrol I needed to drive the 500 kilometre round trip to the airport. By the time I boarded the plane, I was better off than the day I had taken a risk and paid that first instalment. God had not only provided, but he had made available his *abundant* provision. Those months and that experience completely transformed my understanding of God's generous spirit and the ways in which he works. It challenged me to be more generous and to be more readily available to walk in obedience to him, trusting him to provide all that I need along the way.

I personally experienced God come through for me in just a small way, but the lesson and impact on my life was huge. Even now, years later, I often recall that testimony when I am faced with financial challenges. I am reminded that when we walk in obedience and take a risk for God, he blesses us with far more than we ever sacrificed for him. We cannot anticipate or understand the ways through which he works, but we can be sure that he will surprise us.

That first risk, that first step of obedience to pay the first instalment, demonstrated that I was willing to pay the price to follow God's call. That action became the catalyst for God's blessing. All too often we do not take that first step because we fear it will cost us too much, but when we give our all to God, he always returns with more. Our obedience brings breakthrough and leads to blessing.

God knows what we need, when we need it and how to provide it. Sometimes, he gives differently to what we expect. Sometimes, his provision is not financial but relational or circumstantial. Sometimes, he withholds it for a little while to give us time to settle our eyes on him first. But he is not defeated by our needs, as we often feel we are. Our needs are an opportunity for his miracles.

The circumstances that the Israelites faced had looked like a checkmate, but not for God. God never faces checkmate. The rules do not apply to him. His power extends far beyond what we perceive or imagine.

A short time later, after the Israelites had been wandering through the desert for nearly three months (which is just a pinch in the forty years they would live there), they began to complain to Moses about their lack of food. They argued that they would rather have died as slaves in Egypt with full bellies than die of hunger, but free, in the desert.

God told Moses that he would rain down bread, called manna, from heaven and instructed the Israelites to collect only what they needed to feed themselves and their families for that day. Moses pointed out to the people that their complaining was not against him, but against God. But God had heard their moans and promised to provide food for them daily. This would demonstrate to the people that he was the one true God and that he could, and would, provide for their needs.

Each morning, as the sun rose, the heat evaporated the morning dew and left behind the thin, flake-like manna that God had promised. The people collected what they needed for that day, ate and were satisfied. Yet some were disobedient to God's instruction to take only what they needed for that day and kept aside a little extra. By morning, however, the bread that had been saved from the day before smelled and had bred worms.

God then instructed the people to collect twice as much on the sixth day so that they were provided for on the Sabbath, without renouncing the day of rest. On the Sabbath, the extra bread that had been collected the day before remained appetizing and nutritious. And yet some were disobedient then, too. They ventured out of their tents on the morning of the Sabbath in search of food, but they found none.

For forty years the Israelites were provided for in this way. For forty years God met their needs, one day at a time. They were entirely dependent on his provision and his remembering of them. But he did not fail them once.

We may not be on a forty-year pilgrimage through the desert, but God calls us to live this way too. "Saving for a rainy day" is not encouraged in God's kingdom. He seeks to meet our needs every single day, just one day at a time. God does not forget, and he does not run out of food, or money, or clothes, or shelter. When we submit to him and call on him to meet every need, he is faithful to hear us and to respond.

Kathy Keller, wife to pastor and author Timothy Keller, stated: "God doesn't give hypothetical grace for our hypothetical nightmare situation. He only gives us grace for our actual situation."[19] So there is no point in us becoming concerned over how our needs may (or may not) be met in weeks, months, or even years to come. God will meet those needs when they arise, *if* they arise. For now, he is only interested in your needs for *today*. Let him know what they are: what you are anxious for, what bills need to be paid, what decisions are playing on your mind. *He* is our daily provision. *He* is our daily bread. For with him comes everything else.

Oswald Chambers once wrote: "To trust in the Lord is to be foolish enough to know that if we fulfil God's commands, he will look after everything."[20] Our *understanding* is not a condition upon which God decides whether or not to act, but our *obedience* is.

During my search for an apartment when I first moved to Germany, I got caught up in a rental scam. It would seem that they are quite common. They used beautiful photos of an apartment, it was offered for a very reasonable monthly fee, and they claimed to use a well-known website for money transactions. However, as emails went back and forth and I trod carefully down this path of interest, I continued to pray for wisdom.

I eventually identified that it was a scam and was able to end all communication without parting with any money or personal details. It was a frustrating and disappointing set of circumstances, yet God had still been present throughout; he had not let me down or allowed me to get hurt or shamed. Sometimes, he takes us far enough down the track so that we can see his hand at work, but never so far that he can't step in and save us.

When I lived at home with my parents, I wanted for nothing because my dad provided for us. I didn't need to worry about where the money, or food or rent came from; I just enjoyed it. And isn't our Heavenly Father just like that? Does he not also take care of his children? We need only receive it.

But society teaches us to save, and to invest, and to protect our assets, does it not? Shouldn't we be ensuring our pension payments are in place so that we are provided for in retirement? Well, yes and no. God calls us to steward well what he has already given us (Proverbs 21:20), but that should not come at the expense of our dependence on him (Luke 16:10–13, 1 Timothy 6:17–19). We must be careful not to become so entangled in the pressures of the financial climate that we forget who our real Provider is. Malachi 3:10 reminds us to put God to the test by giving generously to his kingdom and to then watch him pour out his blessings upon us. Money, wages, pensions, savings, investments are all just methods through which God may choose to work. Then again, he may also choose not to. Our hope should be in him, not in the means by which he works.

Remember, walking with God is an entirely foreign concept to the world. God's way often contradicts what the world expects us to do; we should be careful not to become so complacent in the world that we lose sight of what God is asking us to do.

For many, one of the biggest hang-ups is the desire to be a people-pleaser. Well, here's the truth: Jesus was no people-pleaser, and we shouldn't be either. We are called to love people, but our aim is to please God.

When the apostle Paul wrote to the church in Galatia, he warned them not to listen to those who adjusted the gospel for their own selfish gain or, perhaps, to ease their own conscience. He warned them: "For am I now seeking the approval of man, or of God? Or am I trying to please man? If I were still trying to please man, I would not be a servant of Christ" (Galatians 1:10).

Notice that we can only do one or the other: please human beings or please God. We cannot do both, for those very desires often contradict one another. If God is pleased, we need to stop worrying about who isn't.

When we run after his best for us, it is inevitable that we will leave people behind. Relationships with friends or even family members who do not understand our convictions may begin to drift. This is one of the most difficult sacrifices, perhaps, that we are called to make in our pursuit of him. But God remains faithful and present, and he will provide us with meaningful relationships and people to run with us as we continue to chase after him.

Matthew 19:29 promises that everyone who has left houses or brothers or sisters or father or mother or children or lands, for his name's sake, will receive a hundredfold and will inherit eternal life. We cannot allow emotions or earthly connections to hold us back from fulfilling God's call on our lives. But in God's economy, the blessing *always* far outweighs the cost, whether in this life or the next.

People may think we look foolish, but few have made a difference in this world without appearing to be so. Seek wisdom from mature believers and weigh everything up against the Word of God, but don't let the opinions or ideas of others hold you back. Resist allowing the voices of others to define who you are. Fix your eyes on your Shepherd and Guide, and faithfully follow his footsteps.

Our priority must be to simply walk in obedience to God, and he will provide everything else that we need. Being part of a community is vital, but be careful to choose people who will encourage you, build you up, support you and urge you ever closer to Jesus. The good intentions of others are to be carefully considered and prayed over, but God's Word has the final say.

Be encouraged by the testimonies of others, and be inspired by what God has done in their lives, but don't fall into the trap of thinking that just because God worked in a certain way in someone else's life, he will work the same way in yours. God is the Creator; he invented creativity so give him space to be creative in your own life. Trust him without borders and give him free reign to do a new thing in your life, something he has never done before.

Isn't the creativity and diversity of humanity beautiful? Does creation not declare the beauty and glory of a loving Father? Why do we try so hard to all look the same when we were carefully and purposefully designed to be *unique*? We need to shrug off the opinions and expectations of others, the fear of what they think of us or the mould they try to squeeze us into. When we embrace the life God has for us, it will not look like any life before it. What matters is that which God asks us to do, not what others expect us to do. There will be people who don't get it, and maybe even people who try to stop you. But let God deal with them; you just focus on being the best version of who God made you to be.

When adventure becomes a habit, peace and contentment become routine, because we learn to be satisfied with each day as it comes. We anticipate great things in the future, absolutely, but we do not forget to enjoy and savour the present.

When we pursue peace, we inherit an abundant life. The distractions that once occupied our minds no longer plague us because we rest assured in the divine sovereignty of God. If we learn to correctly adjust our attitude, the uncertainty in life, once an ordeal, becomes an adventure! Pastor Bill Johnson said: "You don't get the peace that passes understanding until you give up your right to understand."[21]

When we truly recognize who God is and how he loves us, we will be content with whatever path he takes us on, because we understand that his will for us is more secure, more exciting, more fulfilling than anything we could achieve ourselves.

This life, this adventure that you are living, is a journey: a process. It is not a single point in time, a destination, a goal; it is every insignificant moment in between. Don't waste them. Don't miss the minutes because you are too busy counting the hours. Allow God to open your eyes to what he wants to say and do in each second, for only then will life become a crazy, exciting, fascinating, awe-inspiring adventure.

Committing every day to God—every moment, every decision, every opportunity—is the only way to truly live a full and abundant life. It calls for us to live a life of consistency and perseverance. It requires that we live a life of progress, not perfection.

When we learn to live one day at a time, we reach a tipping point. Here we are, sat at the top of the rollercoaster, and this is where the thrills and excitement of faith really kick in. We have no idea what happens next, but we are assured that life with God is so much better than life done any other way. No matter what our needs or our struggles or our battles are, this is where we are meant to be. This is what we were created for. Let's throw our arms in the air and enjoy the ride. Here it comes!

11

The Greatest Adventure

It was an ordinary week: nothing special about it. My nine months of language classes had come to an end, but I had no clue what to do next. I had wanted to continue with further language study, but the cost of the lessons had immediately ruled out that possibility. "I should find a job, I suppose," I had thought. But how? And where? What could I do that would earn me enough money but not require a high level of German?

I had been in Germany for ten months by this point, and I was no closer to figuring out what God's next step for me was. I had obeyed him in moving to Germany to learn the language and culture, but he hadn't given me any further instruction, at least nothing that I could act upon in the coming weeks, or even months. Instead, all he was talking to me about was where he would take me in years to come. ("All good stuff," I surmised, "but how do I get there? And how does that help me now?")

That week, as I began to fret and plead with God for some sort of direction whilst weighing up and taking steps towards the limited options that I had before me, I felt him prompt me to develop my blog. "OK," I thought, not sure how that would help earn me money or further my German language, but at least it was something to focus my mind on.

A few days later, God prompted me to text a friend whom I hadn't spoken to for a few weeks, just to check in and see how he was doing. "OK," I thought, not sure what that had to do with figuring out my next step.

The following day, God prompted me to go to church (on a Friday) to serve refugees in the outreach cafe, only to arrive and find that the gates were locked and no-one was there. I had spent a few precious euros on the tram fare, so I was a bit disgruntled at what seemed to be a waste of time and money. "OK," I concluded, "am I just beginning to make this stuff up? Am I so desperate for direction that I am convincing myself that these random ideas are from the mouth of God?"

With doubts and questions, I made my way back home, only to receive a response a short time later from the friend I had texted the day before. "I don't know why," it read, "but I just thought that you should watch *The Ultimate Gift*."

Um, OK . . . Another random prompt.

And yet, I was already feeling aimless, so what did I have to lose?

Michael O. Sajbel's movie *The Ultimate Gift* follows the journey of Jason Stevens, an arrogant twenty-something with a strong sense of entitlement who expects to receive a hefty inheritance when his grandfather passes away. However, in order to receive the inheritance, Jason must first carry out a series of seemingly pointless and random acts overseen by his grandfather's lawyers.

Among other things, he is tasked to build a fence on a Texan ranch, make a new friend, and act as library assistant in a small Ecuadorian village in South America. Though, at first, Jason's attitude is one of frustration and animosity, with every completed task his heart changes a little more, and he begins to receive the greater, hidden gifts that his grandfather intended for him: the value of work, of friends, of family, of love, of learning, of problem solving, of dreams, of laughter, of gratitude and of generosity.

Upon finally completing the tasks outlined by his grandfather's will, Jason receives the promised inheritance sum of $100 million, only to give the entirety away to a charity that has grown close to his now tender heart.

Jason could not understand why his grandfather had left a series of seemingly odd and aimless tasks to do, but he gritted his teeth and reluctantly got on with them, with his eyes fixed on the promised $100 million. Little did he realize that each task would teach him something far more valuable than any money he could earn, and would prepare him to handle the pledged fortune well. Each task, though apparently unrelated to his final goal, paved the only path that would lead him to his inheritance.

I, like Jason, had begrudgingly followed what appeared to be a series of unrelated and meaningless tasks that week, as directed by God, but I could not understand what they had to do with my next steps. Yet this movie painted a much bigger picture for me; it reminded me that the tasks that God asks us to do are not always what they appear. We may look at the acts themselves, but God's purpose is to use these exercises to change our hearts. He uses every small act of obedience to prepare us for a far greater inheritance that is waiting for us up ahead.

By the time Jason had earned the expected $100 million, his heart and character had changed so much that he willingly surrendered the entire fortune for a far greater cause. Yet, his grandfather had one more, far bigger surprise . . .

The lawyers recognize the pure man that has been birthed through Jason's obedience to his grandfather's wishes, and they award him an inheritance far beyond anything he previously imagined or had his hopes set on. Having been trusted with little (relatively speaking!) he had earned the right to be trusted with much, and received the full inheritance of $2 billion.

At that time, during that period of transition, my eyes were only looking at the small picture and at the steps directly before me. I had asked God small questions and was waiting for small answers. But God had another plan: a bigger plan. He was preparing me for something much grander. While I was impatient and doubting the relevance of the series of tasks he had set out before me, focused on earning myself the "$100 million prize"—that is, the spiritual inheritance that *I* could imagine—God was beginning to prepare my heart and character to receive the unimaginable $2 billion inheritance that was beyond anything I could ever anticipate.

The Bible says: "No eye has seen, nor ear heard, nor the heart of man imagined, what God has prepared for those who love him" (1 Corinthians 2:9). Are you, like I was, so distracted by the inheritance that you can *see*, that you miss the far greater inheritance that God wants to give you? Are you willing to follow his prompts, even if they seem nonsensical and without purpose? Will you trust him and partner with him in the far greater story he is carefully and elaborately piecing together in your lifetime?

Let me ask you: how fit is your imagination? Is it limber and toned, or has it grown stiff and stifled from too much common sense?

I have had to learn to exercise my imagination somewhat, to allow room for my dreams to take root. Being a natural problem solver, my mind would automatically source a path from problem (or idea, or dream) to solution (or reality, or practice) without me even having to ask. But if a path was not easily found, the dream was immediately rejected. I later identified this as a fault in the system.

Through faith experiences and over time, I gradually learnt to override this malfunction in my mind. I learnt to identify where the idea had stemmed from before deciding what to do with it. You see, any dream planted by God was not to be rejected so hastily, no matter how impossible it seemed. A dream planted there by me, on the other hand, was to be pushed aside for it was too puny, too insignificant, too small compared to the dreams that God wanted to manifest.

Any dream we seek to fulfil ourselves is not even worth embarking upon, for it is achievable alone, in our own strength. But God-inspired dreams—those that appear utterly impossible—are the only dreams worth chasing. Michelangelo said: "The danger is not that our aim is too high and we miss it, but that it is too low and we reach it." When dreams are realized, our passion, our drive, our ambition relaxes, and life returns to a mediocre chore. But chasing after God's best will *always* have us reaching out for more. There is no limit, no ceiling, no end to what he wants to do in us and through us.

Before I applied for the Metro World Child internship, another incredible opportunity presented itself to me: to teach in an international school in Uganda. The school had contacted me directly and invited me to work with them for the next two years; all I had to do was say yes.

But I couldn't.

I had already been asking God which step to take next, so receipt of this email had definitely piqued my interest. Uganda had weaved through my thoughts somewhat in previous years, and teaching was a skill I carried. Yet that was not enough. Call me crazy, but it almost seemed a little *too* easy; they would pay me a monthly salary, reimburse the costs of my flights, provide me with housing and even provide some of my meals. The bottom line? It was well within my comfort zone.

I do not seek to belittle the ministry that that school was (and probably still is) doing in that part of the world; it seemed a great school doing a fantastic work. But it was not right for me. It involved very little dreaming (for me), very little dependence on God (for me), and I could already map out a wide path from A to B. I did not seek comfort and ease, where provision was readily available; I sought faith adventures, crazy dreams and impossible-without-God outcomes. I wanted to be tested and tried and to see God do a work in my own heart as I leaned fully on him. It wasn't worth pursuing unless it scared me in the natural, unless that nervous, warm excitement and anticipation bubbled up inside, knowing only God could see me through.

When our decisions or movements take people by surprise, it is either foolishness or God. When we act quickly and seemingly without preparation, it is either foolishness or God. When our lives follow a curve ball and head in an entirely unexpected direction, it is either foolishness or God. When we are rooted in the Word of God and following the convictions of the Holy Spirit in our hearts, our lives will inevitably raise eyebrows.

The journey that God takes us on to fulfil his dreams for us rarely looks normal to anyone else, yet when we step out in faith, he never fails to meet us there. He honours our obedience and invites us to participate in adventure with him.

Don't let those dreams in your heart die because *you* do not know how to bring them into reality; instead trust the One who does. If he planted that dream in your heart, you can be sure he will see it through if you allow him to. Fight the doubt, fight the fear, fight the sound of sense that threatens to steal it away and stand firm on the promises of God. Do not settle for a life less than the one you are capable of living.

The dreams in our hearts, or the open doors of opportunity, or the call to a specific role, will not be possible without him. Our participation in those things will fail unless we partner with God. It's not something he wants *us* to do; instead he's saying, "Hey, I'm going to do this incredible, miraculous thing. Want to come along for the ride?" He asks us to partner with him, to work alongside him, to depend on him and to trust him. You can't reach your destiny alone, because the only available path to get there is in the arms of God.

God is not limited by our own imagination. He is able to do far more abundantly than all that we ask or think (Ephesians 3:20), so dream as big as you can then watch him exceed it. Until the vision you have received from God is realized, you will never be satisfied with anything less.

In the 1950s and 1960s, the race was on as the United States and the Soviet Union competed head-to-head to be the first to send a man to space. Then on 12 April 1961, Yuri Gagarin from the Soviet Union became the first human to orbit the earth, leaving a dejected United States in second, and last, place. Intent on leading his nation to reach the moon first, President J. F. Kennedy gave a rousing speech before 40,000 people at Rice University Stadium in Houston, Texas, eighteen months to the day after Gagarin had touched the stars. "We choose to go to the moon," Kennedy said. "We choose to go to the moon in this decade and do the other things, not because they are easy, but because they are hard, because that goal will serve to organize and measure the best of our energies and skills, because that challenge is one that we are willing to accept, one we are unwilling to postpone, and one which we intend to win."[22]

Kennedy sought to inspire his country to rise up and do hard things: things that had never been done before. He knew that only with great risk is there great reward. He understood that only outside of our comfort zone is there great victory. And when we push the boundaries of what seems possible, we inspire others to follow in our footsteps.

About a year before I left everything behind and moved to Germany, I prayed a risky prayer. I had no idea what God would do, or where he would take me, or what he would ask of me, but I was no longer content living a life within my comfort zone. I had dreams in my heart that had lain dormant for many years, and I could ignore them no longer. I knew I could never expect to do anything worthwhile for God in my own strength, so I surrendered everything to him again:

> God, help me to live a greater life of adventure, of faith, of radical trust in you. Not focusing on or hindered by control, preparation, finance. Help me to fall in love with you again; to desire to spend time with you; to know and understand your ways; to experience adventure, surprise, intrigue with you. Help me not to get caught up or "filter" what you say through my own needs and desires, but to simply love you and pursue you. God, this is a big prayer! I can't do any of it without you. Help me, stand by me, lead me,

guide me, provide for me, give me peace, encourage me, refine me, draw me close to yourself once again.

Reaching the moon was not within America's comfort zone. It was not easy. It was not cheap. It required sacrifice, out-of-the-box thinking, and risk: great risk. It required people, like Kennedy, to stand up and declare the impossible, to encourage others to dream the unimaginable with the few who believed it could be done. Are you ready to aim for the moon? Are you willing to do what has never been done before? Or are you comfortable remaining in your own familiar atmosphere?

Complacency breeds in our comfort zone, but God does not call us to a life of safety, free from pain or challenge. Indeed, the only way to develop courage and faith is to step forward *despite* the fear we carry. If we did not feel the fear, we would neglect to lean on God. He calls us forward anyway. He asks us to do it afraid.

Our purpose in God's great plan is not dependent on our ability, our talents, our life experience, our qualifications or anything else that the world values. Our purpose is entirely dependent on the words that our Creator speaks over us. But it is up to us how we choose to respond to them.

The enemy will try to dissuade you and discourage you by reminding you of all your weaknesses and failings, but don't let him have the last word. His declarations are those of panic and fear, because he recognizes that his hold on humanity weakens with every step of obedience you take towards your purpose in God's kingdom.

Obeying God in every step—whether a small edge forward or a giant leap, a very natural progression or a seemingly crazy curve ball—you can bet that his plans, his purposes, his ways are far, far beyond anything you could possibly dream up for yourself. There will be easy steps, challenging steps, painful steps, unexpected steps, costly steps, exciting steps. There will be steps that seem boring, or nonsensical, or those that you have to wait a long time for. But with every one, God will prepare you to receive even bigger opportunities just a little further down the road.

Early in my adventure I expended too much energy looking to my own abilities first, and calling on God as a last resort. That method, however, was exhausting, stressful and produced little fruit. Today, my first response is to expect a miracle, and to ask him what action he wishes me to take in collaboration with how he will act. By relinquishing the burden of carrying concerns and seeking solutions, his hand has become far more evident in my everyday reality, and the peace and assuredness that I have received is liberating. I do not always get the miracle I ask for, but I am confident that I receive the best solution from God, regardless of what I expect it to look like. Peace, I have learnt, is only available when you lay every aspect of your life into his hands and trust him to act as he pleases.

There will, of course, be times in life when things don't go the way you hope or expect them to. Times when pain, or disappointment, or delay threaten to steal your joy and knock you off track. No individual called by God to do something great will escape great trial and pain, but do not allow that to deter you, for God is faithful. You will never invest more in him than he will in you. The more we rest in God's purposes, the better equipped we are to deal with the losses. Sometimes it is necessary to grieve the loss of what you hoped would be, but do not let that hold you back from the greater thing that God is preparing for you. Pick yourself back up, fix your eyes on him and embrace all that he leads you to.

On this adventure, God wants to not only reveal to us his will and purpose for our lives, but he seeks to lead us by his ways. What I mean by that is that he not only shows us the promise, and pledges to take us there, but he wants to take us by the route he has carefully mapped out. He longs for us to take each step with him. He desires an intimate relationship and daily conversation with us. He hopes that we will humble ourselves and ask for his input so that he can reveal his glory in incredible ways. He does not only reveal himself by his Word, but he delights in showing himself through his Son, Jesus Christ, and through his earthly sons and daughters so that we can experientially know and understand how loving, generous, kind, invested, caring and capable he is.

This adventure that we embark on is a delicate partnership between our responsibility and God's sovereignty. We should exercise wisdom in all aspects of life, yet God takes our choices, both good and bad, and uses them for his glory. No matter the mistakes we make, the opportunities we miss, the steps we fail to obey, God can work our mess into a masterpiece if we only allow him to.

When God has a purpose to fulfil, nothing can thwart his plans:

> When God's in it . . . it flows. When the flesh is in it . . . it's forced.
> . . . If he is in it, it's remarkable how approval will be granted, how a growing interest will percolate, and how the timing will fall right into place. It will come together almost in spite of you.[23]

" . . . in spite of you"—does that not bring with it a huge sigh of relief? God will work, *in spite* of our failings, *in spite* of our disobedience, *in spite* of our fear and doubt. God knows very well that we are not perfect, and he does not expect us to be, so we should not place that unrealistic expectation on ourselves either. He offers us grace, and it is necessary for us to show ourselves grace as well.

We can step forward in peace, for the journey on which we go is under the eye of the Lord. As we remain by his side, he will uphold us with his mighty hand (Isaiah 41:10). Nothing can knock us off course, but ourselves. We must be diligent in seeking him and remaining faithful to him, and our lives will be an adventure, a joy-filled, surprising, abundantly blessed adventure that far outreaches our own limitations. Few stories illustrate this better than the narrative of Joseph, in the book of Genesis.

Joseph was the eleventh of the twelve sons born to Jacob, but he was his father's favourite. Jacob did not hide this fact, instead adorning Joseph with a robe of many colours, causing Joseph's ten older brothers to despise him.

While still only a teenager, Joseph had two dreams, each depicting his father and brothers bowing down to him. Naturally, hearing this only incited his brothers further and they plotted to kill him. However, Reuben, Joseph's eldest brother, convinced the others to throw him into a pit instead, thinking that he would return later and rescue his young brother and bring him safely back to their father. But before Reuben could carry out his plan, his other brothers sold Joseph to a caravan of Ishmaelites on their way to sell their wares in Egypt. In this moment, Joseph's circumstances may have looked (and felt) bleak, but this was God's way of positioning Joseph exactly where he needed him.

Once in Egypt, Joseph was sold to a man named Potiphar, an officer of Pharaoh. I doubt Joseph would have chosen this situation for himself, yet he did choose to be present in the circumstances he found himself in, and to faithfully serve Potiphar and his household, earning the trust of his master. God caused all that Joseph put his hand to to succeed, and Potiphar promoted Joseph to oversee all that he had. Because of God's blessing on Joseph's life, Potiphar and his household were blessed too.

Meanwhile, Joseph had caught the attention of Potiphar's wife. Day after day, she sought to seduce him, but he refused, saying, "because of me my master has no concern about anything in the house, and he has put everything that he has in my charge. He is not greater in this house than I am, nor has he kept back anything from me except yourself, because you are his wife. How then can I do this great wickedness and sin against God?" (Genesis 39:8–9).

Joseph could have felt betrayed and abandoned by God, having been sold into slavery in Egypt. He could have resented the dreams that God had given him, that caused his brothers to act so terribly towards him. He could have thrown his hands in the air and renounced his faith, choosing to rebel against the God who had allowed such injustice to happen to him. But he didn't. Despite everything, he continued to place his hope and trust in God.

Potiphar's wife persisted, but Joseph continually refused to sleep with her. And one day she could tolerate his rejection no longer; she lied to her husband and told Potiphar that Joseph had tried to force himself on her. Potiphar was furious. Feeling betrayed and humiliated, he threw Joseph into jail with the king's prisoners.

Poor Joseph. His circumstances now appeared to go from bad to worse. Yet even here, having been wrongfully imprisoned, God remained with Joseph and opened up doors of opportunity for him in the unlikeliest of places. The prison guard put Joseph in charge of all the prisoners and he was given free rein over how he managed the inmates. Even there, in the darkest corners of the kingdom, God caused everything that Joseph did to succeed (Genesis 39:23).

A short time later, two members of the king's court entered the prison: the king's cupbearer and the king's baker. On the same night, they each had a dream that disturbed them, and they shared their dreams with Joseph the following morning. God gave Joseph the discernment to correctly interpret their dreams, and three days later everything that

Joseph said would happen came to pass; the baker was put to death, and the cupbearer was reinstated in the courts of Pharaoh. As the cupbearer left his cell, Joseph asked him to tell Pharaoh of his innocence so that he could be freed too, but the cupbearer quickly forgot about Joseph.

For another two years, Joseph remained in prison. His family, Potiphar and the cupbearer may have all long forgotten him, but God had not. He continued to quietly and purposefully prepare Joseph to receive the fulfilment of his own childhood dreams.

Then one night, Pharaoh also had a dream that caused him to break out in cold sweats. Upon waking, he consulted all the magicians and wise men in his kingdom, but none could interpret his dream for him. In a moment of inspiration, the cupbearer recalled what Joseph had done for him long before, in the bowels of the palace, and he shared his testimony with the king.

Pharaoh immediately called for Joseph and told him the dream, and once again God gave Joseph revelation and the ability to warn the king of Egypt of what was to come: seven years of great harvest in the land, followed by seven years of famine. He informed the king that he should appoint men to oversee the harvest in the years of plenty, so that it could be appropriately rationed and stored as provision for the impending famine.

This proposal pleased Pharaoh. "Since God has shown you all this," Pharaoh told Joseph, "there is none so discerning and wise as you are. You shall be over my house, and all my people shall order themselves as you command. Only as regards the throne will I be greater than you" (Genesis 41:39–40). At thirty years old, Joseph was appointed chief over all of Egypt, with only the king carrying a greater rule than he. His adventure, his journey, his unrivalled road had led him here.

For over ten years, Joseph had first been positioned, then prepared and finally promoted to the calling and destiny that God had created him for. He had survived rejection, served faithfully in the unseen, overcome injustice, and used the gifts and insight that God had given him to help and encourage the few around him. But because he proved his character and integrity in the small, hidden places, God promoted him to the second most powerful position in the whole Egyptian kingdom. Joseph's compassion and honour had been demonstrated to the few, and consequently God used him to save the nation, and beyond, from starvation.

As the years of famine hit, Joseph's brothers travelled from Canaan to Egypt to buy food, for the famine had reached them too. Upon their arrival, they fell at Joseph's feet and bowed to him, but failed to recognize their brother, whom they had long presumed dead. In that moment, Joseph remembered the dreams that he had had as a teenager that depicted his family bowing down to him. Suddenly, unexpectedly, a dream that God had given him decades before was now the reality he witnessed before him.

As a teenager, God had given Joseph a dream (in his case, quite literally): a vision of what his future would be. Had he believed it? Had he accepted and taken hold of the fullness of that dream? We don't know for sure. But I'd imagine, along the way, he doubted if he would ever see it manifested. Perhaps he assumed it was rather a metaphor or sign of something far less significant that God might do in his life. I bet, from the bottom of the pit or from within a prison cell, the true manifestation of his dream had seemed like an impossibility.

Joseph's journey was one of isolation, and of being misunderstood, of injustice and neglect. But God was always present. God never left Joseph, even in the midst of his challenging and unfair circumstances, and God showed Joseph favour in the small moments. Seeing his dream become a reality perhaps seemed hopeless to Joseph, but he still trusted God and, in his own weakness, depended on God's strength and wisdom. In the middle-moments of his life, when nothing grand or exciting seemed to be happening—indeed, they were bleak by any standards—Joseph allowed God to speak through him to the few that he encountered. And no matter the season, no matter the circumstances, Joseph remained a man of good character and of integrity. In the hidden places, Joseph proved himself as God prepared him, so that, at the right time, God could promote Joseph to a position beyond anything he could have imagined or achieved for himself. He had proved that he could be trusted with little, and therefore God entrusted him with much.

Has God given you a dream or vision that seems so unlikely? Perhaps you are feeling forgotten, misunderstood, unseen. Don't despise these small beginnings (Zechariah 4:10), for at the proper time you will reap a great harvest if you do not give up (Galatians 6:9). Just keep putting one foot in front of the other and God will meet you there.

This quote from Oswald Chambers' book *My Utmost for His Highest* paints a grander picture of what our lives could be:

> If you yourself do not cut the lines that tie you to the dock, God will have to use a storm to sever them and to send you out to sea. Put everything in your life afloat upon God, going out to sea on the great swelling tide of his purpose, and your eyes will be opened. If you believe in Jesus, you are not to spend all your time in the calm waters just inside the harbour, full of joy, but always tied to the dock. You have to get out past the harbour into the great depths of God . . . [24]

At some point we need to cut the ropes that have us tied to the dock, and set sail for open ocean. No-one but God can give you the coordinates of your next anchorage because no-one but you is going there. We can learn from the testimonies of others, and from the great biblical heroes of faith, yet none but God can direct you on your unique adventure to all that he has purposed you for.

When we live our lives filled with purpose and confident of God's hand in every detail, we will fully embrace today and all the potential that it carries, using eyes of faith to anticipate and take hold of the opportunities for miracles. We will permit God to interrupt our day to draw our attention to his work, even when it interferes with our own plans.

I was struck by something Mother Teresa once said: "I have never had clarity; what I've always had is trust. What do you find yourself expressing more consistently to God—your need for clarity or your expression of trust?" When we pray, do we ask God for clarity, or do we simply proclaim our trust in him? Faith is built on trust, not clarity. My prayers have changed since I read this statement. Instead of pleading with God to answer my incessant questions, I choose now to declare my confidence in him and remind myself of who he is and how he loves me. My desire is to trust God wholeheartedly, and I will welcome the clarity he deems necessary to provide, when he chooses to provide it.

We walk forward often in the absence of clarity, but trusting that God will show us where he wants us to go next, and to provide everything we will need to get there. One step at a time, we embrace the adventure that he takes us on. We live so fully in each moment that joy and peace reign, no matter what the circumstances are around us. There is little thought wasted on what is still to come, for it will come in time, but for now we drink in every emotion, every flutter of the Holy Spirit, every sense of what God is doing at this moment. For this moment will pass, never to be repeated, so do not miss the chance to celebrate it, learn from it and to experience God in it.

In chapter 1, I shared that Hebrews 11, with its list of men and women who did great things for the kingdom of God, has always fanned the flame of passion and ambition in my heart. But there was nothing special about these individuals in and of themselves. They were sinners, just like you and me. They made mistakes, just like you and I do. They did not feel qualified or ready, but they acted in faith nonetheless. They did not consider themselves to be heroes, yet the miracles that were birthed from their obedience won them a place in the Hebrews Hall of Faith. They received a standing ovation in heaven because they humbly trusted God and allowed him to use them in whichever way he chose. These faith heroes offered to God what was costly to them but what was acceptable to him. They lived in a way that pleased God and were rewarded, often uniquely, by him. They were obedient to God in response to sometimes outrageous requests, but God healed them, protected them and saved them because of their faith. They left what was familiar and comfortable to embark on a journey to an unknown destination, yet inherited all that had been promised to them. They received in faith what was humanly impossible, and saw the manifestations of those promises. They faced tests and trials and proved their faith genuine, choosing to trust God above all else, even when their circumstances were dire. They left spiritual legacies for their children and the generations that would follow them. They held tightly to their convictions and roots, even when faced with opposition or threatened with death. They recognized God as the King over all kings, the Leader over all leaders, and looked to him over earthly authorities. They experienced miraculous provision from God that was unavailable to those who did not share their faith. They defeated armies, escaped death, demanded justice. They endured beatings, were imprisoned and some even submitted to death, for the sake of the extension of God's kingdom. They also recognized that their time on earth was a mere drop in the ocean compared to the time they would spend with their Father and God in heaven. They did not place much value on their possessions on earth, for they longed for a greater day when they would receive their eternal inheritance. These heroes did not know where God was leading them, but they followed in faith anyway. They listened for their Maker's voice, for his instruction, his way and his timing, and responded in obedience.

Are you willing to be a hero of the faith? Will your obedience earn you a crown and a standing ovation in heaven one day? Are you ready to live out your convictions and see the miraculous work of God in your life? You may not feel like a hero today, but your testimony, your obedience, your adventure may inspire the generations that follow you.

Part of what people find most appealing about adventure is the apparent freedom that comes with it: freedom from responsibility, freedom from relationships, freedom from the daily trudge of life. But true freedom offers us something far greater and is only available at the feet of Jesus. Living in the freedom that Jesus bought for each one of us on the cross should be our greatest desire, for with it comes everything else. Our freedom was bought at such an incredible price that it would be a disgrace not to live in its fullness.

I found true freedom in discovering who God has made me to be. He revealed to me his will and purpose for my life and spoke words of love, acceptance and affirmation over me. As I became more intentional about being quiet and still before him, his voice grew more familiar; as I sought him and his truth, he was faithful to respond. Gradually, my introspective view was no longer about short-term, tangible "jobs" or "roles" that I was linked to, but about *who* I am and what I have to offer to the world and his kingdom, regardless of context.

We know we are truly free when we resist tying ourselves to our own wants or desires. Believing that God has the greatest, most out-of-this-world plan for our lives casts a shadow over all of our meagre dreams, and releases us to live the best life, even when things don't always go the way we want or expect them to.

When we truly accept that his ways trump all others, we can have faith that he will come through for us, that he has heard our prayers and will answer them, and that he will not shame us but protect us and reward our faith. We can be confident, too, in the knowledge that nothing and no-one can frustrate the plans of God. When we are secure in that fact, depending on him to walk with us until the end, no circumstance or challenge can rob us of our peace. We are free to live a life of faith because he loves us so dearly, and he who promised is faithful (Hebrews 10:23).

There is freedom available, too, regarding our material possessions and finances. Not that we should be cavalier in our spending, but we can and should sow into the kingdom and be generous to others, without concern for our own needs. We need to remember that God's economy is not our economy; when we surrender what we have and place it into God's hands, our giving will reach further and impact many more people than we could ever imagine.

One Sunday, not long after I moved to Germany, I was so overcome with joy during the morning worship in church that I desired to empty my purse into the offering bucket and give God everything I had. I had forgotten, however, that that particular week I had received a three-figure reimbursement sum from my language school, so my purse was significantly fuller than usual! Yet I did not hesitate—I did not need to—I gave in worship to my Father who deserves everything. *He* is my source and provider, not the cash in my wallet.

I have always given to my local church and, at times, to different mission organizations or charities, but I think this instance was the first time I had given money out of pure love for God. It was not out of obligation, or considering a cause worthy enough to receive it, or with any thought of how the money might be spent. I did not give a moment's thought to how I might miss the money that I had been so delighted and surprised to receive just a few days previous. It wasn't a *practical* decision—it wasn't about the money—it was about giving everything to the One who has given me everything. In that moment, I knew I was truly free and surrendered to God with a sincere love and adoration for him.

Being assured of the truth that we were created for a purpose and designed with intentionality, finding identity and value in who we are and whose we are, and recognizing God's phenomenal love for us that promises to provide for us, guide us and care for us, allows us to freely obey God in all that he asks us to do. Living in the knowledge and acceptance that you have been appointed and set apart for a unique purpose, receiving the approval of God, is so liberating!

There is a common misconception that obedience to something or someone means surrendering your right to freedom and joy. That may be true of some things, but not of God. Obedience to God is the surest way to freedom and joy. Nothing, I repeat, *nothing*, is more fun than faith!

When we throw ourselves into all that God calls us to, we experience the joy of unimaginable possibilities, of timely and abundant blessing, of self-growth and breakthrough. The risks we take fan the flame of our faith. The challenges we face reveal to us, and God, what is truly inside of us. The attitude we hold reflects in what and in whom we believe. Our relationship with God is one to be enjoyed and savoured. In him we find love, pursuit, comfort, surprise, encouragement, fun. We are free to bask in his beauty and share every precious moment with him. When we keep God as our number one priority, and love him—not just for what he can do for us, but for who he is—our fear, our challenges, our doubt, our questions all pale in comparison. Chase after him! Find him, and in him, everything else.

And when God speaks, it will be time to move forward, to take action, to take everything you have learnt and prepared for and put it into practice. Every experience, every answered prayer, every miraculous circumstance that God has used to pave your journey so far, is all in preparation for where he is taking you now.

Do not misunderstand me; you can begin living your adventure today without any circumstances in your life changing. You do not need to quit your job, or find a spouse, or start a ministry to enter into the adventure God has for you. He may ask you to do those things in time, but he also may not.

What he does require, however, is a surrendered heart: a heart that is open to promptings from the Holy Spirit to begin that conversation, to offer that lift home, to visit that elderly neighbour. Perhaps the situation you currently find yourself in is the perfect launchpad for all that he calls you to. It is no coincidence that you are in that job, friends with those people, raising that family, living in that neighbourhood. But rather than accepting the normality of these circumstances, seek to understand the heavenly possibilities! This is where your adventure begins. Just imagine what God could do for those people through the vehicle of your obedient heart!

We will all, one day, meet the Lord and give an account for how we whiled away the hours that were given to us. May we, too, live under the declarations of Matthew 25:23: "Well done, good and faithful servant. You have been faithful over a little; I will set you over much. Enter into the joy of your master." I long to hear those words said of me, so I surrender myself to God again today and ask him to lead me round the next bend.

For the grand adventure that he is preparing us for is not just for this life, but for the life to follow. He prepares us for eternity, for never-ending communion with him in heaven. He is using every twist and turn in our journey on earth to refine us, shape us and buff us, fashioning us into a reflection of his Son. When we truly grasp this bigger picture, our pain and challenges and anxiety begin to dissolve into joy.

Simon Peter, Jesus' disciple, who had once denied Jesus for fear of what others would think, later stood and called on the other disciples to follow him in telling others of Jesus. The difference? He now carried the power and the boldness of the Holy Spirit. He finally understood all that Jesus had prepared him for and stepped into the purpose that God had called him to.

A short while later, he wrote to the early Christians:

> I know how great this makes you feel, even though you have to put up with every kind of aggravation in the meantime. Pure gold put in the fire comes out of it proved pure; genuine faith put through this suffering comes out proved genuine. When Jesus wraps this all up, it's your faith, not your gold, that God will have on display as evidence of his victory.
>
> *1 Peter 1:6–7, The Message*

I seek not only to survive this lifetime, but to *thrive*. I want a full and abundant life (John 10:10) and to enter *fully* into the adventure that God has prepared for me. I want to walk in complete obedience to him. I want my faith to be tested, for without a test there can be no testimony. And I want the testimonies of what God does in my life to encourage others in their walk with God, to inspire them to pray bigger prayers, dream bigger dreams, and to take greater risks in faith. What about you?

I want to look back on my life and say that I embraced it entirely, that I was not held back by fear (2 Timothy 1:7) but trusted in God wholeheartedly to do just as he said he would (Romans 4:21). Will you join me?

When we completely abandon our lives to God, he can and will do far more with it than we ever could. Our surrender removes the boundaries and limitations of our own abilities and allows God to write the plot to our adventure. Watch him create in you the person you never thought you could be. Watch him carry you to places you never thought you would go. Watch him work miracles you never imagined were possible. Take hold of that John 10:10 life that he offers freely to you, and embrace the adventure you were created for.

Notes

1. <https://www.lexico.com/en/definition/adventure>.
2. <https://utmost.org/the-brave-friendship-of-god/>.
3. <https://www.desiringgod.org/interviews/does-christian-hedonism-make-joy-an-idol>.
4. Pressman, E. (Producer), Malick, T. (Producer), Heaton, P. (Producer), Hunt, D. (Producer), Wales, K. (Producer). Apted, M. (Director). (2006). *Amazing Grace* [Motion Picture]. United States: Bristol Bay Productions & Ingenious Film Partners.
5. Cunningham, C. (Producer), Jackson, P. (Producer), Walsh, F. (Producer), Weiner, Z. (Producer). Jackson, P. (Director). (2012).*The Hobbit: An Unexpected Journey* [Motion Picture]. United States: Metro-Goldwyn-Mayer (MGM) & New Line Cinema.
6. A. W. Tozer & James L. Snyder, *Experiencing the Presence of God: Teachings from the Book of Hebrews* (Bloomington, MN: Bethany House Publishers, 2010), p. 209.
7. <https://www.mentalhealth.org.uk/statistics/mental-health-statistics-relationships-and-community>.
8. <https://childmind.org/article/how-using-social-media-affects-teenagers/>.
9. Beth Moore, *Believing God* (Nashville, TN: B&H Publishing Group, 2004), p. 64.
10. <https://billygraham.org/about/biographies/billy-graham/>.
11. <https://billygraham.org/devotion/his-timing-is-perfect/>.
12. Lysa TerKeurst, *Am I Messing Up My Kids?* (Eugene, OR: Harvest House Publishers, 2006), p. 208.
13. Cunningham, C. (Producer), Jackson, P. (Producer), Walsh, F. (Producer), Weiner, Z. (Producer). Jackson, P. (Director). (2012). *The Hobbit: An Unexpected Journey* [Motion Picture]. United States: Metro-Goldwyn-Mayer (MGM) & New Line Cinema.

[14] Oswald Chambers, *My Utmost for His Highest: Updated Edition* (Grand Rapids, MI: Discovery House, 1992), July 5 entry.
[15] Elisabeth Elliot, *Through Gates of Splendor* (Carol Stream, IL: Tyndale House Publishers, Inc., 2005), p. 8.
[16] Bill Wilson, *Whose Child is This?* (New York City, NY: Metro World Child, 2012), p. 27.
[17] Elizabeth Elliot, *Shadow of the Almighty* (Milton Keynes, UK: Authentic Media, 2005), p. 185.
[18] John Ortberg, *Know Doubt: Embracing Uncertainty in Your Faith* (Grand Rapids, MI: Zondervan, 2008), p. 137.
[19] <https://www.instagram.com/p/BXmekHbh2kO/?hl=en>.
[20] Oswald Chambers, *Run Today's Race* (Grand Rapids, MI: Oswald Chambers Publications Association Ltd., 1968), October 31 entry.
[21] Bill Johnson, *God is Good* (Shippensburg, PA: Destiny Image Publishers, Inc., 2018), p. 195.
[22] <https://www.space.com/17547-jfk-moon-speech-50years-anniversary.html>.
[23] Charles R. Swindoll, *Great Lives: Moses: A Man of Selfless Dedication* (Nashville, TN: Word Publishing, 1999) p. 57.
[24] Chambers, *My Utmost for His Highest*, 8 June entry.

EU GPSR Authorized Representative:

LOGOS EUROPE, 9 rue Nicolas Poussin, 17000 La Rochelle, France

contact@logoseurope.eu

www.ingramcontent.com/pod-product-compliance
Lightning Source LLC
Chambersburg PA
CBHW050552160426
43199CB00015B/2633